GERMAN U-BOAT ACE
Rolf Mützelburg

GERMAN U-BOAT ACE

Luc Braeuer

Rolf Mützelburg

The Patrols of U-203 in World War II

Schiffer Publishing Ltd

4880 Lower Valley Road • Atglen, PA 19310

Published by Schiffer Publishing, Ltd.
4880 Lower Valley Road
Atglen, PA 19310
Phone: (610) 593-1777; Fax: (610) 593-2002
E-mail: Info@schifferbooks.com

For our complete selection of fine books on this and related subjects,
please visit our website at www.schifferbooks.com. You may also write for a free catalog.

This book may be purchased from the publisher. Please try your bookstore first.

We are always looking for people to write books on new and related subjects.
If you have an idea for a book, please contact us at proposals@schifferbooks.com.

Schiffer Publishing's titles are available at special discounts for bulk purchases for sales promotions or premiums. Special editions, including personalized covers, corporate imprints, and excerpts can be created in large quantities for special needs. For more information, contact the publisher.

CONTENTS

U-203 arrives in Brest on July 29, 1942, returning from its seventh patrol that took place in the Caribbean sector. The conning tower is decked out with oak leaves to celebrate the commander's new decoration. *UBA*

Navy officer Rolf Mützelburg was one of the most emblematic figures of the German U-boat Corps. On June 20, 1941, U-203, which he commanded, was the first U-boat in the blockade zone around England to be confronted by the unexpected presence of an American warship. Ten days later, it was the first to penetrate a concrete U-boat shelter on the French coast. After obtaining regular success against convoys in the North Atlantic during its first four patrols, it claimed new victims at the end of the year off the Canadian coast. To be able to act for an extended period off the U.S. coast during its sixth patrol, on March 24, 1942, U-203 was the first U-boat to be supplied at sea by another U-boat!

In July 1942 in the Caribbean, during its seventh patrol, it obtained its best results. It was always to be found in the busiest sectors before the Allies organized their defenses, which allowed Commander Rolf Mützelburg to win the highest decorations of the epoch and to become an "Ace" of the U-boat Corps. After several successful patrols, he shared, along with Adalbert Schnee, Teddy Suhren and Erich Topp, the rare privilege of being close to Dönitz, who affectionately called them his "Four Aces." Moreover, the Admiral chose Rolf Mützelburg to keep an eye on one of his sons, a cadet in training during the fourth and fifth combat patrols. The crewmembers of U-203 highly respected their commander, nicknamed *Mübu*, and in turn he was close to his men. Together, they obtained good results in each of their patrols.

After St. Nazaire, U-203 that belonged to the 1st Flotilla adopted Brest as its homeport, but it also stopped over several times in Lorient. Rolf Mützelburg followed closely in the footsteps of his friend Adalbert Schnee, both born in the same year, who was the commander of U-201: on January 25, 1941, this U-boat was the first VIIC-type in the 1st Flotilla to be put into service, three weeks before the second, which was U-203!

During that year, Adalbert Schnee was the first commander in the 1st Flotilla to win the Knight's Cross, on August 30, and the thirty-sixth officer of the U-boat Corps to be awarded this decoration. Mützelburg was the second in the 1st Flotilla and thirty-seventh officer to receive it on November 17. When Mützelburg's U-203 arrived in Brest for the first time on September 30, 1941, it berthed alongside U-201 that had arrived just before it! Both men added Oak Leaves to their Knight's Cross

Portrait of Rolf Mützelburg, commander of U-203, taken in the summer of 1942; he wears the Knight's Cross with Oak Leaves around his neck. *UBA*

on the same day, July 15, 1942, and flew together to Germany to receive the decoration. But after that their destinies separated: unlike Adalbert Schnee, who accepted a job on land with the U-boat Corps General Staff, Rolf Mützelburg obstinately refused when Admiral Dönitz offered him a similar job.

He was thus the most highly decorated officer in the German U-boat Corps to take an active part in combat. His desire to remain with his men cost him his life during an accident at sea, which remains unique in the history of the U-boat Corps: because of a swell, he was accidently killed after hitting the saddle tanks while diving from the conning tower. For U-203's later patrols, he was replaced by his former Watch Officer, Hermann Kottmann, who was also highly motivated. This former officer on the *Graf Spee*, scuttled in Argentina on December 17, 1939, had crossed the Pacific to reach Germany and enlist in the U-boat Corps. In spite of the Allies' progress, concerning armament and location that coincided with U-203's departure on patrol at the end of 1942, it carried out three more patrols before being sunk on its eleventh patrol in a combined attack by an Allied plane and a destroyer.

Rolf Mützelburg Is Named Commander of U-203

Mützelburg, named *Leutnant zur See* on January 1, 1936, started his career on minesweepers. He volunteered to join the Submarine Corps in October 1939. *UBA*

S on of a Navy officer, Rolf Mützelburg was born on June 23, 1913, in Kiel. After leaving college in Flensburg, he enlisted in the *Reichsmarine* in August 1932. After graduating from Naval School, he began his career as an officer on minesweepers between November 1936 and April 1938. When war was declared in September 1939, he was the commander of the 12th Minesweeper Flotilla. However, the following month he volunteered for U-boats. On January 1, 1940, during theoretical courses for this corps, he was promoted to the rank of *Kapitänleutnant*.

His training continued during the second half of 1940 with the command of U-10 U-boat School in the Baltic Sea. At the end of November, Rolf Mützelburg was sent to Lorient. He boarded U-100 commanded by the "Ace" Joachim Schepke, to take part in a patrol as commander-in-training, from December 2, 1940, to January 1, 1941. He learned a lot during this patrol during which three ships were sunk.

On the right of the first row of recruits, the young Rolf Mützelburg was nineteen when he entered the *Reichsmarine* in August 1932. Behind him, Helmut Rosenbaum, future commander of U-73, who was awarded the Knight's Cross in August 1942. *UBA*

Arriving in Kiel after the patrol, he found U-203 being built in the *Krupp Germania Werft* shipyards. He became its commander after the putting into service ceremony on February 18, 1941; he was twenty-seven-years-old at the time. The insignia of U-203 was painted on the conning tower: the blazon of Essen, the U-boat's patron town, whose representatives were present at the ceremony. U-203's Watch Officer was *Oberleutnant zur See* Klaus Heyda, the Second Watch Officer *Leutnant zur See* Heinz-Dieter Mohs; the U-boat's Chief Engineer was *Oberleutnant (Ing.)* Heinrich Heep, a Mechanics Officer who took part in the first eight combat patrols. Like all new U-boats, U-203 and its crew followed a three-month tactical training course in the Baltic Sea.

Sent to Lorient in December 1940, Mützelburg carries out his first combat patrol as commander-in-training aboard U-100, commanded by the "Ace" Joachim Schepke. *UBA*

Mützelburg's crew leave for Danzig and Gotenhafen for a three-month tactics course on the U-boat. *UBA*

The insignia of U-203, the coat of arms of Essen, is painted on a plate riveted on the front of the conning tower. *LB*

In March 1941, the U-boat is towed out to sea to avoid a port in the Baltic Sea blocked by ice. *UBA*

U-203 in a protected dock in Kiel. *UBA*

During the ceremony for putting U-203 into service, the crewmembers gather around their commander. Representatives from Essen, the U-boat's patron town, and from *Krupp Germania Werft* shipyard in Kiel that built the U-boat are also present. *UBA*

The Patrols of U-203

FIRST PATROL
TWO CONVOYS ATTACKED ON THE SAME DAY; INAUGURATION OF THE U-BOAT BASE AT ST. NAZAIRE

After training in Danzig and Gotenhafen and an overhaul in its shipyard, U-203 was ready for combat and left on June 5, 1941, for its first patrol in the North Atlantic. After a call in Bergen, between June 7-8 for refueling, it left for the Atlantic but had to turn back the next day, due to a problem with seawater leaking into the portside diesel engines.

After being repaired, it left the Norwegian port definitively on June 11, heading west. During the five days it took to reach the south of Iceland, it passed north of the British Isles and had to dive on numerous occasions following the appearance of planes, or the sighting in the distance by the watch crew in the conning tower, Royal Navy ships. On June 18, U-203 reached the AK according to the German charts dividing the Atlantic into squares; this position was midway between Canada and England.

U-203 leaves the port in Kiel on June 5, 1941, for its first combat patrol. *UBA*

Leaving Kiel in the wake of a sweeper to avoid mines, the U-boat, commanded by Mützelburg, heads for Bergen Port in Norway. *UBA*

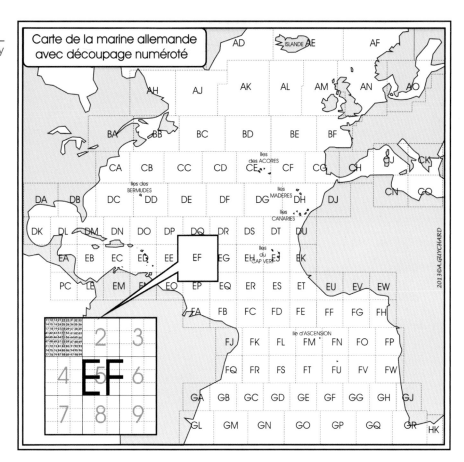

Map showing the Atlantic divided into squares used by the Kriegsmarine. *Drawn by Anthony Guychard*

Carte de la marine allemande avec découpage numéroté

It was here, in the early hours of June 20, that the watch crew in the conning tower spotted a destroyer escorting an American warship, identified by the commander as the USS *Texas*. The German U-boat watched it for several hours, wondering what an American warship was doing in the blockade zone around Britain where it wasn't supposed to be. At 13:07, a radio message signaling its presence was sent to the U-boat Corps Command, which replied: *"Don't attack it!"* If the presence of an American battleship in this sector violated international conventions, the *BdU* didn't want an incident to interrupt America's neutrality at that time. Moreover, two days later, as U-203 continued west to carry out its patrol, the loudspeaker on board announced that Germany had declared war on the USSR.

Five days are needed to arrive in the AK square midway between Canada and the British Isles, the position fixed by the Submarine Corps Command. This is where the American battleship USS *Texas* was found in the early hours of June 20, in the middle of the blockade zone around Britain; the battleship wasn't attacked. *LB*

Preparing meals for the forty-five crewmembers in the U-boat's tiny kitchen. *LB*

While the watch crew scrutinize the horizon, Midshipman Günther Drescher smokes a cigarette and chats with *Bootsmaat No.1*, Ernst Heimann. *UBA*

On June 23 at 13:20, the watch crew in the conning tower what they had all been waiting for: convoy in sight! A radio message was sent to the *BdU* to signal the convoy's position: AJ 9253 square, direction: 060 and its speed: 10 knots – it was the HX-133 convoy out of Halifax on June 16 heading east for Liverpool, with fifty-one merchant ships. All that day, U-203 tracked the convoy at a distance; it spotted an auxiliary cruiser with two smokestacks, several cargo ships, and a destroyer to protect them. At two o'clock on the morning of June 24, the commander decided to attack on the surface. At 03:31, after closing to a distance of 600 meters from his target, he ordered the launch of two torpedoes at the auxiliary cruiser and two others against a large cargo ship estimated at 8,000 tons and which also had two smoke-stacks, and then they crash dived and moved away, seeing the closeness of the destroyer. Two detonations were heard. The commander believed that he had missed the auxiliary cruiser but had sunk another cargo ship in the convoy sailing behind it, estimated at 5,000 tons, as well as the 8,000-ton cargo ship they had aimed at. In reality, only the 4,402-ton Norwegian cargo ship *Soloy* carrying wheat was hit and it sank in fifteen minutes. Its entire crew survived and was picked up by another ship. While it was submerged, U-203's four front torpedo-launching tubes were reloaded; the U-boat wasn't attacked by depth charges.

On June 23, 1941, a convoy is sighted and the commander orders a crash dive! In the Control Room, these men maneuver to empty the air ballasts so the U-boat can dive. *LB*

Sketch taken from U-203's logbook of the attack on June 24 at 03:31 against two merchant ships escorted by a destroyer in the HX-133 convoy. Only the Norwegian cargo ship *Soloy* was hit and sunk. *UBA*

It resurfaced at 06:00 but the convoy was no longer in sight. The U-boat was forced to dive several times to try to find the direction the convoy had taken using the hydrophone. All of a sudden, while the U-boat was on the surface, the crew noticed the exterior valve of the port-side Diesel engines' exhaust tube was broken. This meant that the U-boat could no longer dive to any great depth and would be more vulnerable to depth charges. However, the commander decided to continue his patrol, hoping that the next convoy spotted wouldn't have too many escort ships to protect it.

At 06:45, a new convoy was spotted in the distance, and the U-boat closed on it. This was the OB-336 convoy with twenty-four ships heading in the opposite direction to the previous convoy, out of Liverpool on June 15 bound for the North American coast.

Two hours later, U-203's watch crew in the conning tower spotted U-79 commanded by Wolfgang Kaufmann that was also hunting the convoy. At 10:15, U-203 arrived alongside the convoy and the commander decided to attack the medium-sized cargo ships opposite him as the escort ships were obviously occupied elsewhere! Approaching, he ordered four torpedoes to be launched from the front tubes; the sea was rather rough. The first torpedo missed, but the second torpedo hit a ship estimated at 6,000 tons, right in the middle, breaking it in two.

The third hit another cargo ship estimated at 5,000 tons that seemed to sink, the fourth missed its target. At 12:25, the U-boat dived to reload its torpedo tubes while following the convoy.

The diesel engine's exterior exhaust valve is broken; the U-boat can't dive to any great depth. *Yves Rio*

In reality, only one cargo ship was sunk during this attack, the 4,956-ton British *Kinross*, whose entire crew of thirty-seven men was rescued.

The third attack of the day began at 14:42; two torpedoes were fired in direction of two ships in the convoy and U-203 immediately dived and moved away. Because of the rough sea, it was impossible to see the results through the periscope. Because the diesel engines' exhaust valve was broken and ten torpedoes had been fired, the commander decided to head back to the French coast. A radio message was sent to the U-boat Corps Command at 20:20 announcing their return, their damage, and a score of four ships sunk for 24,000 tons. On June 26, U-203's radio operator deciphered a radio message from the *BdU* telling U-203 to head for the port in St. Nazaire.

During the morning of June 24, the port-side diesel engine develops a problem! *UBA*

Sketches of the two series of torpedoes fired against OB-336 convoy: above, lancing four torpedoes from the right flank; below, firing two torpedoes and then turning back. *UBA*

The British 4,956-ton *Kinross* was sunk during U-203's first attack. *DR*

After firing ten torpedoes, the commander orders the return to the French coast. On June 24, a message announcing his return is sent to the *BdU* that, two days later, replies with a message telling him to head for St. Nazaire. Watch crews take turns without pause during the crossing of Biscay Bay; on the left Ernst Heimann, on the right, Second Watch Officer Heinz-Dieter Mohs.

While chasing a second convoy, U-79, which is also hunting, is sighted. *UBA*

KINROSS

Two young German women have brought bouquets of flowers for Commander Mützelburg. *Kapitänleutnant* Udo Heilmann, commander of U-97, gives them technical explanations about the U-boat. *ECPAD*

On June 29 at 09:00, the U-boat met up with its escort off St. Nazaire. It arrived at 12:30 where it was met in the lock by several Navy officers and two young women with bouquets of flowers. The Chief of the 7th Flotilla's General Staff, *Kapitänleutnant* von Vreeden boarded U-203 to welcome the crew. He then gave the commander some astonishing news: the following day, U-203 would be the first U-boat to penetrate one of the first three operational pens in the completely new U-boat base in St. Nazaire!

Vizeadmiral Karl Dönitz, Chief of the U-boat Corps, as well as the engineer Fritz Todt, whose organization had been in charge of the construction of the first three pens and had completed the work in less than six months, would be present to welcome them, as well as the press and the cinema news reporters. Putting into service the first concrete base in France, three months before the shelters in Lorient, whose port had been open to U-boats since July 1940, was a great event! A ceremony during which the *Organisation Todt* would turn the base over to the *Kriegsmarine* had been planned.

The welcoming ceremony is over; the crewmembers can relax and smoke a cigarette. On the left, in white summer uniform, is war correspondent Lothar-Gunther Buchheim, future author of *Das Boot*. *UBA*

On June 29, 1941, U-203 enters the lock of the port in St. Nazaire. *UBA*

In the conning tower, Commander Mützelburg salutes the welcoming committee lined up on the quay. *UBA*

Kapitänleutnant von Vreeden, Chief of the General Staff of the 7th U-Flotilla, followed by Commander Mützelburg and a war correspondent, salutes U-203's crew. *UBA*

U-203 entered the base at 11:00 on June 30, 1941, with four victory pennants fixed to the periscope. Above the concrete roof whose wooden coffers hadn't yet been removed, hundreds of German workers from the *Organisation Todt* and the base's shipyard greeted U-boat singing *"Wir fahren gegen Engeland"* (We sail to take on the English). Inside the pen, which hadn't yet received its equipment, Dönitz introduced Commander Mützelburg to Fritz Todt, who was wearing the uniform of a *Luftwaffe* general. Once the U-boat was sheltered, the crew and its commander were taken by bus to *La Baule* sea resort where a hotel and a good bath awaited them. The crew was given ten days' leave under the hot July sun.

Commander Mützelburg has been given bouquets of flowers as a welcome to St. Nazaire gift. The Chief of the General Staff tells him that the following day, he and his U-boat will take part in inaugurating the U-boat base! *UBA*

Inside the base, Dönitz introduces Commander Mützelburg to Minister Fritz Todt, a former pilot in the First World War, who is wearing a *Luftwaffe* general's uniform. *ECPAD*

It's a happy moment for the crew: they receive their mail that has accumulated since their departure the previous month! Most of the men have had a shave before their arrival and they are wearing garrison caps with the insignia of their U-boat: the coat of arms of the town of Essen. *UBA*

U-203's logbook with the details of the first operational patrol was signed by Godt, the Chief of the *BdU'*s General; this first operation with a new commander and a new U-boat, was considered very positive. U-203's four victory pennants indicated 8,000, 5,000, 6,000 and 5,000 tons for a total of 24,000 tons declared; in reality, the score in this first patrol was two ships sunk for 9,358 tons. On July 1, Commander Mützelburg was simultaneously awarded the Iron Cross 2nd Class and 1st Class, which he pinned to his white summer uniform. Indeed, the Iron Cross 1st Class couldn't be awarded if the Iron Cross 2nd Class hadn't been won.

The commander of U-203 joined the commanders of the 7th Flotilla in the port in St. Nazaire to welcome and congratulate Erich Topp, who was awarded the Knight's Cross during his last patrol. Then they took part in the inauguration of the exposition of German sea painters whose theme was U-boats. This exposition, installed in *l'hôtel Royal* in La Baule, had been mounted by the war correspondent s based in La Baule-les-Pins commanded by Schwicht and seconded by a certain *Leutnant* Lothar-Günther Buchheim, who, after the War, wrote the famous book "*Das Boot*" ("The Boat") in which he recounted his patrol aboard U-96!

Standing on the rear end of the U-boat, a war correspondent films the putting into service of the first base of this type on the French coast. The submariners came to call this base the "Grand Central." *LB*

Between the two attacks against the OB-336 convoy, U-203 dives. *Yves Rio*

On June 30, 1941, at 11:00 hours, inauguration of St. Nazaire's first three pens. U-203 maneuvers in the dock, with four victory pennants for the ships announced sunk during its first patrol. In the background: the hangars of the *Compagnie Générale Transatlantique* and the customs barracks. *LB*

U-203's crew, lined up on the bridge, pass in front of the stand holding *Vizeadmiral* Dönitz and Minister Fritz Todt, whose organization was in charge of building the base. *LB*

First Patrol: Two Convoys Attacked on the Same Day; Inauguration of the U-Boat Base at St. Nazaire

This photo was on the front page of the German magazine "*Die Wehrmacht*." The shelters at Lorient weren't operational until September. *LB*

Above the concrete roof, whose wooden coffers haven't been removed, hundreds of German laborers from the *Todt Organization* and the base's shipyards welcome the U-boat by singing, "*We're leaving to fight England.*" *LB*

Later, these first pens were numbered 6, 7 and 8; they were in the center of a base containing fourteen pens. *LB*

On July 2, 1941, Mützelburg leaves La Baule sea resort with several other officers and waits on the quay of St. Nazaire's lock to welcome Erich Topp, who has just been awarded the Knight's Cross. *UBA*

On July 6, dressed in white summer uniforms, several commanders and officers belonging to the 7th Flotilla take part in the inauguration of the exhibition of German sea painters held at *l'Hôtel Royal* in La Baule. On the right, Lothar-Gunther Buchheim; with the micro, Lieutenant Schwicht, Head of War Correspondents in La Baule, and Commander Mützelburg. *ECPAD*

At rest in a villa in La Baule before the departure on July 10. Commander Mützelburg, with the Iron Cross 1st Class received on July 1 pinned to his breast pocket, chats with his radio operator, *Funkmaat* Heinz Bald. *UBA*

Departure for the second patrol! They say goodbye to those staying behind. *UBA*

After the broken exhaust valve had been repaired, new torpedoes and foodstuffs were loaded, and U-203 left St. Nazaire on July 10, 1941. A war correspondent had boarded with the crew to take photos.

Five days after its departure, the U-boat reached the patrol zone that the *BdU* had given it by radio, the BE 1550 square; another message was received in the evening sending it to a destination farther north. The U-boat covered around 150 miles a day. Arriving in the AL 7250 square on July 17, a new message signaled a convoy spotted by a *Condor* further south. U-203 headed in that direction on the surface at full speed. By midday it had covered 278 miles in twenty-four hours. After diving several times to listen for propeller sounds, the convoy couldn't be found.

At midday on July 21, an event broke the patrol's monotony: the watch crew spotted a large, isolated steamer in the distance. Its speed was estimated at twenty miles and it zigzagged endlessly. For the rest of the day, at top speed, U-203 tried to get into firing position.

Oil is loaded aboard U-203 at the beginning of July 1941, in St. Nazaire. *UBA*

Passing through the lock on July 10, 1941. *UBA*

Finally at 20:56 the steamer disappeared into the fog. The convoy spotted by the *Condor* several days earlier, and searched for by a whole line of U-boats spread out in a rake across the Atlantic, was finally spotted by the Italian submarine *Barbarigo*. At one in the morning of July 23, the *BdU* transmitted its new position by radio, the CF 8989 square. U-203 continued its route south. On July 26 at 18:08, a radio message finally signaled that U-68 had sighted the convoy in the BE 5838 square. U-203 wasn't far away, and detonations were heard after 22:30, probably torpedoes and anti-submarine depth charges. At 02:19 on July 27, the convoy was reached! This was the OG-69 convoy comprising twenty-seven ships out of Liverpool on July 20 for Gibraltar with a very heavy escort.

On board everything was prepared for action: at 02:52, three torpedoes were launched from tubes No.1 to No.3 in the direction of large cargo ships; the first two were hit in the middle, but the third torpedo malfunctioned. The two cargo ships hit were estimated respectively at 6,000 and 8,000 tons. A fourth torpedo was launched from tube No.4 against a cargo ship weighing 7,000 tons, but the torpedo didn't explode. After this last fire, the U-boat stayed on the surface to reload its tubes, remaining at a distance to keep an eye on the convoy. All of a sudden, a destroyer emerged out of the night and headed directly towards U-203, whose conning tower was caught in the ship's spotlights! Crash dive!

Seven depth charges exploded while the U-boat was only at a depth of forty meters; two and then nine other charges exploded very close to the U-boat, tossing it about as it dived deeper. After two hours searching with ASDIC, the two destroyers still in the area gave up the chase. The attack score wasn't good: only the 2,475-ton British cargo ship *Hawkinge* carrying coal, had been sunk by Mützelburg's torpedoes.

On July 21, 1941, a steamer is spotted in the distance. U-203 tries to get into firing position Günter Gräbnitz (*a.k.a.* Bobby) pushes the diesel engines to their maximum. But at the end of the day, the ship disappears. *UBA*

Chef Rudi Köhler prepares the meals. *LB*

The trash is thrown overboard. *LB*

During the first ten days of the patrol, no ships are seen. Helmsman Hans-Jürgen Haupt checks their position with the sextant. *LB*

Meal in the officers' quarters. *LB*

Five days later, U-203 reaches the zone where the OG-69 convoy had been spotted. *LB*

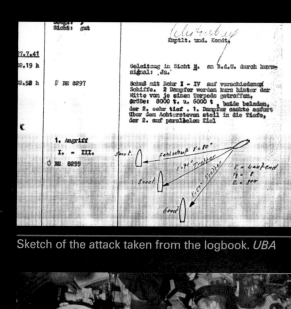

Sketch of the attack taken from the logbook. *UBA*

At 02:52, three torpedoes are launched in the direction of the large cargo ships; two explosions are heard. *LB*

The British ship *Hawkinge*, victim of U-203, sinks in the middle of the night. *LB*

The U-203 resurfaced at six o'clock in the morning; smoke from ships was spotted at 08:13. But eleven minutes later: alert! A destroyer was heading directly towards the U-boat, forcing it to dive. The destroyer stayed in the area for three hours. However, the convoy was spotted once again at 15:00 and the commander decided to wait until dark before attacking a second time. However, at 23:30, the convoy was lost with the arrival of huge black clouds and fog. During the entire morning of July 28, U-203 sailed south; at 14:17, it met U-126 and then at 14:30, the smoke from the convoy was spotted once more. This time, to avoid losing it in the smoke at night, the commander decided to attack during the day. All afternoon, U-203 approached the convoy, which finally emerged out of the fog on its port side at 20:17! It was heavily protected by several destroyers and even by a seaplane perhaps a Sunderland. The commander let the two destroyers at the head advance, as well as a third protecting the convoy's port side, which passed just above the U-boat.

Second Watch Officer Heinz-Dieter Mohs drinks from the special cup, reserved for successful firing. *LB*

With the arrival of a destroyer that catches U-203's conning tower in its spotlight, the U-boat immediately dives. The electric motors are turned on by the mechanics, Schneider and Kurt Ulmer. *LB*

The 1,330-ton British cargo ship *Lapland* is one of the two victims of U-203's second attack against the OG-69 convoy. *DR*

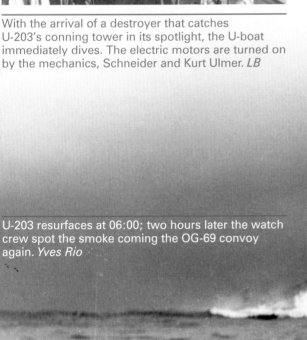

U-203 resurfaces at 06:00; two hours later the watch crew spot the smoke coming the OG-69 convoy again. *Yves Rio*

During the day of July 28, U-203 is positioned in front of the convoy to attack it in the obscurity. The commander gives the order to dive, to let the escort destroyers pass above them. *UBA*

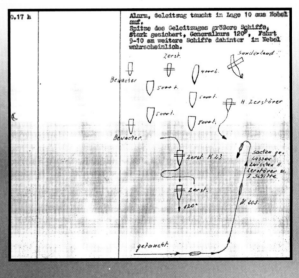

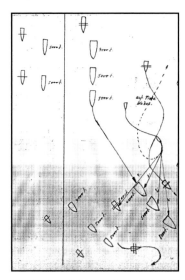

The U-boat fires four torpedoes from its front tubes towards three cargo ships, before diving and moving away. Two explosions are heard! *UBA*

The fuel tanks are getting low after several days on the surface sailing at top speed and Commander Mützelburg decides to head back to the base. *LB*

U-203 approaches St. Nazaire. *UBA*

A total of six pennants, a red one for a warship and five white ones for the cargo ships, have been raised on their arrival in St. Nazaire. In reality, only three ships have been sunk for a total of 5,321 tons. *UBA*

Rolf Mützelburg, in front of the victory pennants, he hasn't shaved during the patrol. Above his left breast pocket he is wearing a metal silhouette of a U-boat, which he allows his men to wear if they have taken part in at least two combat patrols under his command. *UBA*

The U-boat then surfaced and fired its four front tubes, as usual from a distance of 600 to 800 meters, in the direction of three cargo ships estimated at 8,000, 5,000, and 4,000 tons and one at one of the leading destroyers. It dived immediately and heard the four torpedoes exploding, and then two other explosions and later the characteristic sound of ships sinking. Now it was payback time: thirty-two depth charges were dropped by the escort ships that had turned back to chase U-203. However, in spite of ASDIC, the U-boat managed to escape them. During the attack, only two cargo ships had been hit sunk, the 1,330-ton British *Lapland* transporting tin plaques, and the 1,516-ton Swedish *Norita* with a cargo of coal.

U-203 resurfaced July 29 at 00:58. After the days of full speed on the surface, it had just enough fuel to return to its base. It turned back and arrived in St. Nazaire on July 31 a 14:00 flying six victory pennants, including one for the battleship declared sunk during the last attack. The accumulated tonnage of the cargo ships on the five victory pennants totaled 31,000 tons, which was an enormous exaggeration of the truth: only three ships had been sunk for a total of 5,321 tons. This difference between the commander's estimation and the tonnage really sunk was regularly noticed in the logbooks, particularly in the event in a night attack on a convoy: often forced to dive immediately after the torpedoes had been launched to escape from escort ships, the commander estimated the results of his torpedoes uniquely from the sound of the explosions heard on the hydrophone, which often caused errors of calculation, sometimes huge errors.

After its arrival in St. Nazaire, the crew spent several days of R&R in La Baule, where on August 4, Commander Mützelburg was interviewed by a war correspondent for the German radio.

Helmsman Hans-Jürgen Haupt smokes a cigarette in the conning tower. *LB*

Chief Engineer Heinrich Heep, rarely seen in the conning tower, has let his beard grow during the patrol, so that on arrival no one will be in any doubt that he belongs to the U-boat Corps. *UBA*

On July 31, off St. Nazaire, U-203 meets up with U-95 commanded by Schreiber, which follows it into the port. *UBA*

Mützelburg is welcomed on the quay in St. Nazaire by several officers of the 7th Flotilla. Opposite him, the commander of U-751 Gerhard Bigalk, and on his left in white uniform Heinrich Lehmann-Willenbrock, commander of U-96; both of them will be leaving on operations on August 2. With a total of 68,000 tons of ships declared sunk in two patrols, Commander Mützelburg is approaching the 100,000 tons necessary to be awarded the Knight's Cross. *UBA*

The U-203 left St. Nazaire for its third patrol on September 20, 1941, with *Kapitänleutnant* Hans Gilardone on board as commander-in-training. On September 25 at 22:15, a convoy, signaled by the *BdU,* was spotted by the watch crew in the conning tower after five days at sea, in the BE 4176 square. The convoy was mostly made up of small ships and a few larger ones, well protected by escorts. This was the HG-73 convoy out of Gibraltar on September 17 for Liverpool, with twenty-five merchant ships.

The commander decided to attack two high tonnage ships that were in the middle of the convoy; one of them appeared to be a 12,000-ton petrol tanker. At 00:31 on September 26, U-203 fired four torpedoes from its front tubes. It dived as soon as the first detonation was heard. While under the water, three other explosions were heard. The two ships sunk were the 3,442-ton British *Avoceta*, a British liner carrying Convoy Chief Rear-Admiral K.E.L. Creighton.

Commander Mützelburg directs leaving maneuvers. In the foreground in blue uniform, are Watch Officers-in-training: on the left Cadet Günther Drescher, on the right *Leutnant zur See* Rudolf Dübler. For this patrol, U-203 also has a commander-in-training: *Kapitänleutnant* Hans Gilardone. *UBA*

French civilians watch the U-boat leave the port; for security reasons, U-203's insignia on the front of the conning tower has been painted over. *UBA*

U-203 in the lock at St. Nazaire. *UBA*

On September 20, 1941: preparing to leave.St. Nazaire. Watch Officer *Oberleutnant zur See* Klaus Heyda checks that the equipment is present and correct. *UBA*

Losses on board were heavy: forty-three crewmembers, four artillerymen and seventy-six passengers were killed. The others, including the admiral, were picked up by three other ships, notably the *Cervantes* that pulled three men out of the water. However, this ship was sunk by U-201 commanded by Schnee the following day; the three survivors from *Avoceta* who were on board were saved a second time and taken to Liverpool. The second ship sunk during the initial attack was the 2,842-ton Norwegian cargo ship *Varangberg* carrying 4,100 tons of iron ore.

Hit by two torpedoes on its side, it sank immediately, taking its commander and twenty crewmembers with it. The U-boat was chased by an escort ship that launched twenty-six depth charges at about 1,000 meters from the U-boat.

Three hours later, U-203 surfaced. The watch crew spotted four rescue ships in the area where the targeted ships had been, as well as an escort ship and the tanker which had been fired at; it had stopped and its crew was being evacuated. At 06:34, after firing three torpedoes at the destroyer, which missed it, the fourth fired at the tanker hit it in the middle, and it sank in three minutes. The third victim of U-203 wasn't a petrol tanker but the 1,348-ton British cargo ship *Lapwing*; only nine of its crewmembers survived. At 14:02, the U-boat was forced to dive when a plane appeared, and then found the convoy once again at 16:00 in the BE 1676 square; a message signaling its position was immediately sent to the *BdU*. At 22:00, while U-203 was getting ready to fire at a cargo ship, the ship was torpedoed by another U-boat! On September 27, at 00:32, U-203 fired two

Crewmembers help out in the kitchen. *LB*

Serving the meal. *LB*

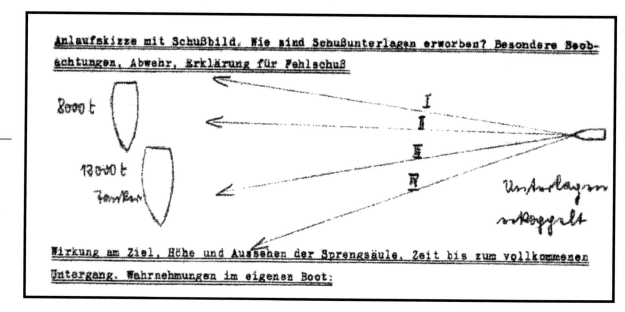

After five days at sea, U-203's watch crew spot a convoy in the BE 4176 square. At 00:31 on September 26, four torpedoes are launched in the direction of two large ships, which sink. *UBA*

torpedoes at medium sized cargo ships, while at a depth of two meters and from a distance of 1,500 meters, to avoid the escort ships; it missed both targets. During the day it was forced to dive four times, following the appearance of Allied seaplanes, probably Sunderlands. However, it continued to track the convoy that was sighted again at midnight.

On September 28 and 29, it was forced to dive on numerous occasions, and then the commander decided to turn back for their home base. This time, a radio message from the *BdU* told him to go to Brest, the new homeport for the 1st Flotilla's U-boats. At midnight, the watch crew sighted U-201 commanded by Schnee in the BF 1903 square; they arrived one after the other at 14:00 in Brest. During this short patrol, the commander declared sinking two ships, an 8,000-ton cargo ship and a 12,000-ton petrol tanker. In reality, he had sunk three ships for a total of 7,632 tons. The day after their arrival in Brest, a decoration awarding ceremony was held in front of the former French Naval

After taking a third victim in the convoy, on September 29 Commander Mützelburg decides to turn back. The *BdU* sends a message telling him to head for his new homeport in Brest. After the action, everyone eats together, from left to right: Mützelburg, "Achmed," Heimann, Second Watch Officer Heinz-Dieter Mohs and Chief Engineer Heinrich Heep. *LB*

School, which had been requisitioned and which had become the new HQ of the 1st U-Flotilla. Its chief, *Korvettenkapitän* Hans Cohausz, handed out the Iron Cross 2nd Class to deserving crewmembers of U-203, notably the two Cadets Rudolf Dübler and Günther

For his culinary talents, Chef Rudolf Köhler is wearing a homemade decoration with two soup spoons crossed above a star that has the profile of a U-boat drawn on it. During their stay in Brest, U-203's crewmembers don't often leave the naval school where their canteen, situated in the middle of the buildings, offers plenty of distractions and low prices, especially for beer and cigarettes. This is where they hold farewell parties before leaving on patrol. When they cross the Penfeld to go into town, they go to the *Café de la Marine*, the bar *"Le Mimi"* and the club *"Le Bouchon,"* whose sign is a large, golden champagne cork; inside, the lamp shades are also shaped like champagne corks! *LB*

U-203 and U-201 arrive together in Brest on September 30, 1941. The commander of U-201, Adalbert Schnee, who has already been awarded the Knight's Cross, is given the honor of berthing first. He salutes his friend Rolf Mützelburg, who will berth alongside. *UBA*

Drescher, who had finished their Watch Officer training course after three combat patrols. These two cadets weren't the only men to disembark, Watch Officer Klaus Heyda left for the Baltic Sea to become Watch Officer aboard U-580; he was killed during exercises at sea in a collision with a German ship on November 11, 1941. He was replaced on U-203 by former Second Watch Officer Hans-Dieter Mohs, whose place was taken by former Helmsman Hans-Jürgen Haupt, who was given the grade of Midshipman. Commander-in-training Hans Gilardone also disembarked; he took the command of U-254 aboard which he was killed on December 8, 1942.

German nurse Gretel offers a bouquet of flowers to Commander Mützelburg. *UBA*

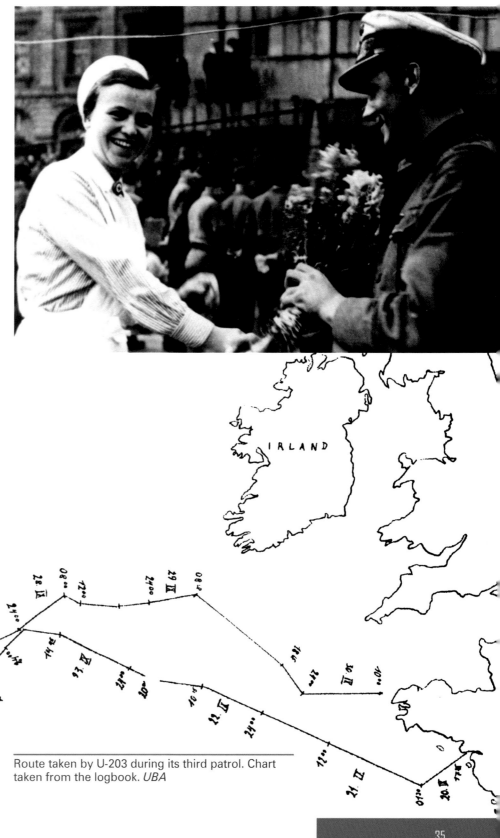

Route taken by U-203 during its third patrol. Chart taken from the logbook. *UBA*

On October 18, 1941, U-203 left Brest for its fourth combat patrol. Cadet Peter Dönitz, the son of the Commander-in-Chief of the U-boat Corps, was on board to take part in two patrols as Watch Officer-in-training. The U-boat was heading for the AL 51 square, to the west of Ireland. During the day of the 19th, it was forced to dive several times because of the sudden appearance of a Sunderland seaplane. At 20:00 the following day, the radio operator deciphered a message telling them to head for the AJ 6496 square, further west off the point of Greenland, where a convoy had been signaled by U-84, commanded by Uphoff. However, on October 21 at 17:00, a message from Hardegen, commander of U-123, signaled another, closer convoy towards the south, in the BE 2131 square; this one was made up of twenty-two ships escorted by three warships. Commander Mützelburg decided to head for this zone at full speed.

On October 18, 1941, U-203 leaves the U-boat base in Brest for its fourth combat patrol. *UBA*

For this winter patrol, Commander Mützelburg, like the rest of the crew, has been given a great leather greatcoat while in Brest. *Yves Rio*

Watch Officer Heinz-Dieter Mohs. *UBA*

The U-boat crosses the dangerous Bay of Biscay on the surface, the watch crews are particularly on the alert in the event of approaching planes! *Yves Rio*

On October 21, the commander passes the hatchway to announce that a convoy has been located a short distance south of their position. U-203 must surface at full speed. *Yves Rio*

Authorization to come into the conning tower? *UBA*

The convoy was sighted at 18:21 in the AL 9738 square, but a seaplane was constantly overflying it; another U-boat had been discovered and bombed. This seaplane forced U-203 to dive in its turn at 20:00. When the U-boat resurfaced half an hour later, the plane was still visible and it took the watch crew another thirty minutes to find the convoy once more. An attack was planned, but the U-boat had to get into a good firing position. But at 22:10 a destroyer arrived! U-203 dived and the escort launched three depth charges about 100 meters from the U-boat. The destroyer chased the U-boat both on the surface and submerged until 01:30. At 02:15 on October 22, U-203 outdistanced its pursuer and got into a good firing position opposite the convoy; it fired three torpedoes in the direction of a petrol tanker and a cargo ship. But the torpedoes missed their targets; perhaps they were sailing too fast? At 02:34 the U-boat dived to reload its tubes; it resurfaced at 04:21, but the convoy had disappeared. This was the SL 89 convoy, out of Freetown for Liverpool, which only lost two ships, sunk by U-82.

Torpedoes are greased so they glide through the water better. *LB*

Three torpedoes are fired at a petrol tanker and a cargo ship, but they miss their target. *UBA*

On October 22, at 02:15, the U-boat is in a good position to fire, opposite the convoy spotted the previous day. The men are at their posts in the control room. *UBA*

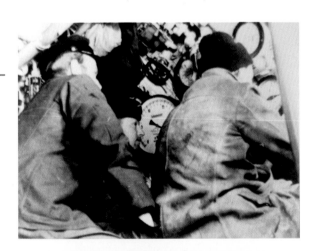

U-203 resurfaces, but the convoy is no longer in sight. The U-boat will have better luck with the next convoy, which is attacked by so many U-boats that it is forced to turn back. *Yves Rio*

They are put into the torpedo-launching tubes. *LB*

At 15:30 a seaplane dived at U-203 and dropped two bombs close by which tossed the U-boat about, causing damage on board: compass and manometers broken, water leaking into the electric engines. The mechanics immediately got to work repairing the damage while the U-boat continued heading west. On October 28 at 13:57, it arrived in the search position fixed by the *BdU*, the AJ 6495 square, opposite the Canadian coast off Newfoundland. U-203 joined the *Schlagetot* wolfpack that was spread out in a rake to find an eventual convoy. On October 30, the line of U-boats was sent further south, and a convoy was discovered two days later by U-374 commanded by Unno von Fischel. The ships in the convoy were also spotted by U-123 on November 2 at 17:40. U-boats regrouped to attack in a pack. This was the SC-52 convoy out of Port Sydney in Canada on October 29 with thirty-four merchant ships which advanced slowly. U-203 spotted it in its turn on November 3 at four in the morning, but lost it in the fog. Four hours later, the U-boat was attacked by one of the escort destroyers, which was quickly joined by a second. The chase continued until the end of the afternoon.

On November 12, at 10:25, U-203 meets up with the escort ship that leads it to Brest. *LB*

On November 18, 1941, a fleet of cars belonging to the 1st Flotilla pass the well-camouflaged kiosk of the former French Naval School. Riding in the first car is Dönitz with Mützelburg, as well as the victory pennants he has brought back from his attack on the SC-52 convoy. *ECPAD*

The U-203 in front of the U-boat base which is overlooked by the old naval school. Note the crew's uniforms drying on the antennae wire. *LB*

At the school, in *cour Jean Bart*, Dönitz salutes U-203's crew. Dönitz's son Peter is the sixth from the left. *LB*

The admiral decorates Mützelburg with the Knight's Cross. This is the second ceremony of this type to take place in Brest, after that for Adalbert Schnee in August 1941. *LB*

Because of the fog and the continued presence of the escort ships, the commander decided to fire blindly in the direction of the convoy from a depth of fifteen meters, following the sound of propellers heard in the hydrophone. Four torpedoes were fired and four explosions were heard, the first two at a distance of 1,800 meters, the two others at 2,300 meters, followed by the characteristic sounds of two ships sinking. The destroyers turned to attack fifteen minutes later; depth charges exploded 1,000 meters from the U-boat and it was chased until 23:00. Two British merchant ships had been sunk by the torpedoes from U-203, the 5,626-ton *Empire Gemsbuck* and the 4,830-ton *Everoja*. The first, which was broken in two, carried 6,200 tons of diverse cargo, including engines, its thirty-six crewmembers were rescued; the second carried 6,401 tons of wheat, its crew of thirty-five were also picked up by a destroyer.

The convoy was attacked by so many U-boats just after its departure, that it was forced to turn back to Sydney after losing four ships; this was a unique case out of the 177 SC convoys bound for Liverpool. On November 5, a radio message from the *BdU* told U-203 to begin its return journey. On November 11 at 14:15, the U-boat was attacked by a Hudson that dropped four bombs rather precisely, causing damage on board on the level of an engine and the depth bars.

U-203 resurfaced at 15:00 but was forced to dive again when the fighter plane was spotted once again at a distance of 8,000 meters! At 17:47 the journey home continued on the surface. The escort, which was to accompany it to Brest, was spotted at 10:25 on November 12, and they reached the port at 14:00. Following Mützelburg's last report, the U-boat Corps Command noted

With his Knight's Cross around his neck, Commander Mützelburg thanks his crewmembers. Together, they have (in theory) passed the 100,000 tons of ships sunk. He makes the following speech: *"Comrades, I thank each one of you for this decoration! I will wear it for all of you, because you, our brave ship and I form a single entity. It's only together that we can fight, win, and survive!"* *LB*

Midshipman Peter Dönitz will take part in one more patrol on U-203. *UBA*

Rolf Mützelburg with the Knight's Cross around his neck. All U-boat commanders dream of being awarded this decoration. *UBA*

A signed photo; he is the 37th Submarine Corps' officer to have been awarded this decoration. *UBA*

that the commander had reached the figure of 100,000 tons of Allied ships sunk. He was awarded the Knight's Cross on November 18, handed to him by *Vizeadmiral* Dönitz in Brest, in the *cour d'honneur* of the former French Naval School. He was the thirty-seventh submariner to receive this decoration; he became henceforth one of the "Aces." The damage sustained by the U-boat during the two plane attacks kept the U-boat in Breast for six weeks. This allowed the crew to go on leave in two shifts. Those who remained in Brest helped the workers in charge of repairing their U-boat.

Der deutsche U-Bootfahrer-Nachwuchs
Kapitaenleutnant Muetzelburg der juengste Ritterkreuztraeger der U-Bootwaffe
Von Kriegsberichter Kurt Schulze

PK. Die hohe, schlanke und straffe Gestalt des Befehlshabers steht vor der Front. Er spricht in militaerisch knappen Worten und Saetzen, die sich in ihrer vorgetragenen Art und Weise zu einer einpraegsamen kurzen Rede formen, dem jungen U-Boots-kommandanten, der gruessend neben seiner Besatzung steht, in direkter Anrede lobende Worte der Anerkennung aus fuer sein tapferes Verhalten, sein kluges wie geschicktes Operieren gegen stark gesicherte Geleitzuege und seinen frischen Angriffsschneid. Es sind Worte, die den Dank des Fuehrers und Obersten Befehlshabers sowie den des ganzen deutschen Volkes an diesen tapferen Offizier ausdruecken.

Vizeadmiral Doenitz, der Vater der U-Bootsfahrer, wie ihn seine Maenner nennen (ein gutes Zeichen fuer eine Kampftruppe, die eine der schwersten Lasten des Krieges zu tragen und haerteste Kaempfe zu bestehen hat), tritt an den Kommandanten heran und legt ihm das Ritterkreuz des Eisernen Kreuzes mit dem leuchtenden Rot des schwarz-weiss-roten Bandes um den Hals. Ein fester Haendedruck, ein herzlicher Handschlag auf die Schulter, der nochmals die Anerkennung des Befehlshabers ausdruecken soll und eine gutmuetige Mahnung: »Nun, Junge, lasst Euch aber nicht vom Hafer stechen!«

Die Maenner koennen ihrem Admiral nicht sagen, dass sie bleiben werden wie sie sind, denn sie stehen eisern still mit Blickwendung zu ihm. Es ist aber auch gar nicht noetig. Wer sollte das nicht besser wissen, als jener, dessen Gedanken immer bei diesen tapferen Maennern sind, wenn seine Befehle sie an den Feind fuehren.

Der Kommandant kann nur lachen. Es ist das Lachen einer stolzen Freude. Jetzt steht er vor der Besatzung, spricht einige Worte, die seinen Dank an die Maenner ausdruecken sollen. Viele Worte sind es nicht. Doch sie genuegen, dass beide verstehen, was den Kommandanten wie auch die Besatzung in diesen wenigen Augenblicken fuer Gedanken und Gefuehle bewegen. Vielmehr vermag unter dem Haendedruck und das kurze Gegenueberstehen mit offenem Blick Auge in Auge, auszudruecken und zu sagen. Das klingt auch nicht nach Phrase. Das ist echt.

Taegliche Zerreissprobe

Kapitaenleutnant Muetzelburg, der juengste Ritterkreuztraeger der U-Bootwaffe! Auf mehreren Feindfahrten hat sich dieser junge Flensburger Kommandant die hohe Tapferkeitsauszeichnung erworben. Seit mehreren Monaten ist er erst mit seinem Unterseeboot an der Front. Es reizt, an den Kaempfen und Erfolgen dieses Mannes und seiner Besatzung die naive Albernheit der Behauptungen fuehrender englischer Minister ueber die schlechte Qualitaet des deutschen U-Bootfahrer-Nachwuchses nur durch die Gegenueberstellung des reinen Kampfgeschehens dieses jungen Bootes in ihrer ganzen haltlosen Erbaermlichkeit und Unwahrhaftigkeit zu enthuellen. Die Bewaehrung der Maenner dieses neuen Bootes

Kapitaenleutnant Muetzelburg

weil ihre physische und pychische Veranlagung sie als U-Bootfahrer bei der Musterung praedestinierte. Der Kern liegt vielmehr dort, wo ihn die englischen Minister nicht zu finden vermoegen, weil sie unseren Worten nicht glauben wollen und aus einem bloedsinnigen Hoffnungswahn so gern an unserer Staerke zweifeln. Es ist die hervorragende Ausbildung des Nachwuchses, der nicht, wie einst bei Beginn des Westfeldzuges jener Tom Chester, nur mit Kriegsgeraet behaengt und dann mit der Parole in den Kampf geschickt wurde: »Boys, you will have a jolly war!« Ein deutscher Offizier an einer Unterseebootsschule sagt seinen Schuelern bestimmt nicht, dass sie einen »jolly war« haben werden; er macht sie vielmehr mit den ernstesten Gefahren des U-Bootkrieges bekannt. Nicht umsonst sind die Lehrer des Nachwuchses bewaehrte Frontkommandanten.

Doch wir stehen nicht an, uns mit leicht aufstellbaren Behauptungen des Mundes zu begnuegen. Die Kaempfe dieses einen Unterseebootes die im Kriegstagebuch des Kommandanten spaeter ja einmal nachgeschlagen werden koennen, sollen den Beweis erbringen, dass der deutsche U-Boot-

fahrer-Nachwuchs taeglich seine Zerreissprobe besteht.

Zum Tauchen ist es zu spaet

Eine tolle Geschichte spielte sich bei einem Nachtangriff auf einen Geleitzug ab. Der Kommandant hatte einen Briten vorgenommen. Es musste nach der langen Back und der Bruecke, die mittschiffs lag, ein Tanker sein. »U..« kommt schnellig zum Angriff an den Tanker heran. Die Muendungsklappen auf und Kapitaenleutnant Mützelburg gibt an dem TO. Feuererlaubnis. Aber ausgerechnet in dem Augenblick als der TO. den Befehl »Rohr los!« geben will, fliegt der Tanker in die Luft. Fluchen kann man zu der spontanen Schimpfkanonade nicht mehr sagen, wenigstens ist keines der Woerter in einem irdischen Lexikon vermerkt.

Natuerlich rief der in die Luft geflogene Tanker Zerstoerer und andere Sicherungsfahrzeuge auf den Plan. Leuchtgranaten schiessen in den Himmel. Da war die Bescherung! Die anderen schiessen und »U..« jagen sie die Zerstoerer auf den Hals. Also runter in den Keller. Die Wasserbomben blieben ohne Wirkung.

Nach einiger Zeit gibt der Kommandant Befehl zum Auftauchen. Er begibt sich sofort auf die Bruecke.

Verfluchter Saukram! Querab kommt ein Zerstoerer heran. Zum Tauchen ist es zu spaet. »U..« geht sofort auf grosse Fahrt. Doch, ist das moeglich, schnitten die da drueben? Das muessen das auftauchende U-Boot gar nicht bemerkt haben. In etwas mehr als 100 Meter Entfernung braust der Zerstoerer an »U..« vorbei.

Kurs auf die Auftauchstelle. Als er genau auf der Stelle ist, gehen die Wasserbomben ueber Bord, die fuer »U..« bestimmt sind. Grotesk! »U..« sieht sozusagen seine eigenen Wasserbomben fallen. Der Tod sprang also hinter »U..« in seinen eigenen Tod.

Doch jetzt hatte der Zerstoerer das Kielwasser von »U..« gesehen. Sofort schiesst er Leuchtgranaten. MGs haemmern, Kanonen bellen. Rings um das Boot liegen die Einschlaege. Die Maenner auf der Bruecke ziehen instinktiv die Koepfe ein. Der Kommandant rettet die ploetzlich ernst gewordene Situation. Durch geschicktes Manoevrieren kommt »U..« vom Zerstoerer ab und kann schnell tauchen. Zwar hagelte noch ein Regen von Wasserbomben herab, aber die Situation war gerettet...

Des oefteren meldete der Wehrmachtsbericht in der letzten Zeit, dass unsere U-Boote Angriffen zersprengten nichtetemm. An einem solchen Geleitzug war auch Kapitaenleutnant Muetzelburg mit seinem Boot. Das war die erfolgreichste Fahrt, sie brachte fuenf Schiffe, und einen Zerstoerer.

Der harte Schlag traf einen Geleitzug. In der Nacht geht der Kommandant zum Angriff ueber und versenkt gleich zwei Dampfer mit 18 000 BRT. Torpedos muessen nachgeladen werden. Aber »U..« bleibt dran. Und als die Arbeit beendet ist, jetzt Kapitaen-

Hunderttausend Tonnen zu Neptun geschickt
Kapitänleutnant Mützelburg mit dem Ritterkreuz ausgezeichnet

Die Nachricht von der Verleihung des Ritterkreuzes zum Eisernen Kreuz an Kapitänleutnant Rolf Mützelburg, dem wagemutigen Kommandanten eines erfolgreichen U-Bootes, hat die Essener Bevölkerung mit Stolz, Bewunderung und Freude erfüllt. Nummer liegt der amtliche Bericht vor, dem wir folgendes entnehmen:

Kapitänleutnant Rolf Mützelburg wurde am 23. Juni 1913 in Kiel als Sohn eines Marine-Stabsingenieurs geboren und trat 1932 in die Kriegsmarine ein. Nach den üblichen Ausbildungskommandos wurde er 1936 zum Leutnant zur See befördert. Er ist zunächst Dienst als Wachoffizier und Kommandant in einer Minensuchflottille. Dann wurde er zur U-Boot-Waffe kommandiert und 1940 zum Kapitänleutnant befördert. Kapitänleutnant Mützelburg hat als Kommandant eines Unterseebootes bisher elf bewaffnete feindliche Handelsschiffe mit insgesamt ca. 100 000 BRT, einen Zerstörer versenkt und außerdem weitere Schiffe torpediert, so daß mit weiteren Schlägen gegen die englische Versorgungsschiffahrt zu rechnen ist. Mützelburg ist ein vorbildlicher Kommandant, der sein Boot mit ausgezeichnetem Geschick und großer Kühnheit führt und der trotz schwerer feindlicher Gegenwehr hervorragende Erfolge errang.

Bereits am vergangenen Sonntag hat Oberbürgermeister Dillgardt dem siegreichen Kommandanten und seiner tapferen Besatzung in einem Telegramm die herzlichsten Glückwünsche der Stadt Essen mit folgendem Wortlaut übermittelt: "Mit mir freuen sich alle Essener über den großen Erfolg und die Verleihung des Ritterkreuzes. Ich gratuliere Ihnen und der ganzen Besatzung im eigenen wie im Namen der Stadt Essen hierzu. In der Hoffnung, daß wir Sie und Ihre Mannschaft bald in Essen begrüßen können und sich weitere Erfolge für Sie anreihen, grüßt Sie herzlichst Ihr Dillgardt, Oberbürgermeister."

Inzwischen weilte Kapitänleutnant Mützelburg zu einem kurzen Besuch in unserer Stadt und wurde von Oberbürgermeister Dillgardt und den Vertretern der Partei und den Spitzenbehörden herzlich empfangen. Auch die Essener Volksgenossen werden bald Gelegenheit haben, "ihren" Ritterkreuzträger und seine tapfere Besatzung zu begrüßen, nachdem Oberbürgermeister Dillgardt die Einladung zu ihrem Besuch bereits ausgesprochen hat. Möge das kämpferische Vorbild des Esseners nahestehenden Ritterkreuzträgers jeden von uns eine nicht nur momentlich unsere Jugend anspornen, in dieser Zeit nur pflichtbewußt und treu zu bleiben. Dann hat der heroische Kampf unserer Helden an der Front seinen letzten Sinn erfüllt.

Kapitänleutnant Mützelburg (Aufn.: van Heekern)

The local newspaper in Essen, U-203's patron town, congratulates Mützelburg and publishes a copy of the telegram sent by the mayor in the name of the town council. *UBA*

War correspondent Kurt Schulze writes an article about the commander's career and describes the medal-awarding ceremony in Brest. He reports that Dönitz had whispered to the commander telling him not to change now, and not to feel superior. *UBA*

A small Christmas tree has been set up on the 88mm gun. *UBA*

With a second Watch Officer-in-training, Midshipman Günter Dobenecker, U-203 left for its fifth patrol on December 25, 1941. A Christmas tree was put on board so that the crew could celebrate the holiday. After the dangerous crossing of the Bay of Biscay, the radio operator deciphered the message received on December 27 at 08:00 from the *BdU* sending their U-boat on patrol in the CF 7585 square, off Gibraltar. The men asked themselves if they would have to pass through the Strait to reach the Mediterranean. At midnight on December 31, 1941, an alarm sounded on board to celebrate the New Year: eight glasses for the old year, eight glasses for the new one! At 00:03 on January 1, the logbook noted: "*surface for the New Year.*"

On December 25, 1941, U-203 leaves the U-boat base in Brest for its fifth patrol. *UBA*

Crewmembers prepare pies and cakes for Christmas night. *Yves Rio*

Mützelburg celebrates Christmas with his crew, around the tree taken on board in Brest. *LB*

The crew is very close to its commander. *LB*

Alert at midnight on December 31, 1941 … Happy New Year! All have a beer. *LB*

A radio message sends U-203 off to Gibraltar; will they have to pass through the feared Strait? *Yves Rio*

Games are organized on board to celebrate the New Year, notably roulette! On January 2, 1942, a radio message orders U-203 along with U-84 and U-552, to head for the Canadian coast! *UBA*

On January 6, 1942, east of the Azores, Chef Rudolf Köhler dives to catch a turtle. *LB*

The turtle is hauled on board – its meat will make an excellent soup. On the right, at the top, is Midshipman Peter Dönitz, one of the admiral's two sons. *UBA*

After several days heading northwest, the sea gets very rough. This submariner, sent to fetch equipment from the foredeck, has been soaked by a huge wave. *YR*

On January 2 at 22:30, a message from *BdU* gave U-boat a new operation sector on the other side of the Atlantic, once again off Newfoundland in the BC 70 square. On January 6, at 16:00 east of the Azores, a huge turtle was spotted in the water. Stunned by a hand grenade, it was hauled on board by Chef Rudolf Köhler. Turtle soup was prepared and the crew decided to make the turtle the U-boat's new insignia!

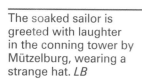

The soaked sailor is greeted with laughter in the conning tower by Mützelburg, wearing a strange hat. *LB*

On January 10, at 21:50 after several days heading west, a steamer with two smoke stacks and two masts was sighted in the BC 8652 square and the U-boat tried to get into firing position, but without success – the steamer was too fast. Another steamer was spotted the next day at 15:25, but the rough sea made an attack impossible once again. At 18:20, the wind got up to force twelve, the sea to force ten and lookout from the conning tower was impossible so the U-boat continued on its route for several hours underwater. On January 12 at 14:26, visibility was good and a destroyer with four smoke stacks was spotted in the BC 7383 square, but the sea was still too rough to attack it. Another isolated steamer was sighted on January 15 at 10:43, sailing at an estimated speed of eleven knots.

This time the sea was calmer, the commander decided to attack and U-203 began its approach. At 11:34, a torpedo was fired from tube No.1, a huge explosion was heard forty-two seconds later – the fuel tank must have been hit and it sank in two minutes. It was the large 632-ton Portuguese fishing ship *Catalina* with a cargo of cod. On January 17, at 08:32, a cargo ship was discovered in the BB 6913 square close to the Canadian coast, south of Cape Breton Island. It was very fast with an estimated speed of fourteen knots. The U-boat maneuvered while the ship zigzagged when suddenly the ship arrived just opposite the U-boat! At 11:21, tubes No.2 and No.3 were fired and the 1,345-ton Norwegian cargo ship *Octavian* sank with its cargo of sulfur and wood resin; the entire crew of seventeen men was lost. In the afternoon of January 17, U-203 continued underwater until it arrived off Cape Race.

In the beginning of January, the closer U-203 gets to the Canadian coast, the sea gets rougher and the temperature is more and more icy. *LB*

The commander has gone into the conning tower to direct fire through the combat periscope. *LB*

Three ships are hit off the Canadian coast during the second half of January 1942; two are sunk and the third is only damaged. *LB*

The next morning, a destroyer was spotted and the commander decided to head out to sea. The U-boat approached the coast again the following night, but no traffic was seen during the day on January 19. Suddenly, at 02:35 the next morning, a rapid steamer was spotted, and as it was at full speed, the U-boat was forced to abandon the chase. Then at 05:35, the watch crew spotted a group of five destroyers! The U-boat headed out to sea at full speed, the sound of the ASDIC could be heard in the distance. Submerged, U-203 approached the Canadian coast once again in the morning of January 21 and the commander decided to follow the coast to St. Johns. At 18:30, a large steamer estimated at 8,000 tons was seen at a distance of 3,000 meters.

The commander ordered the firing of tubes Nos.1-4 and hearing an explosion, declared the ship as sunk. In reality, the Canadian ship *North Gaspe* weighing only 888 tons used by the U.S. Army Transport Service and carrying a cargo of war equipment, had only been damaged by the explosion of a torpedo not far from it; it was able to reach the nearest port. U-203 drew close to the coast again and at midnight discovered several ships at anchor, guarded by destroyers, but it only had three torpedoes left! A double attack was launched against a steamer at 01:10 on January 22 from a distance of 800 meters, but the two torpedoes missed. The U-boat turned raound to fire its last torpedo from the No.4 rear tube. After forty-four seconds, a large explosion was heard, but not from the cargo ship: behind it was a destroyer and the commander thought he had sunk it.

Mützelburg drinks from a silver goblet after the successful torpedoing. *LB*

At 04:00, the commander ordered the return to the home base. He communicated his estimated results by radio to the *BdU*: three ships sunk for 18,000 tons, an escort ship probably destroyed. In reality, his score for this patrol was two merchant ships sunk for 1,977 tons and an 888-ton ship damaged. After crossing the Atlantic from west to east, the U-boat base in Brest was reached at 14:00 on January 29, 1942. In addition to its four pennants, the turtle's shell was hung on the periscope for the arrival, and even the Christmas tree loaded at the departure was put on display. A new insignia was painted on the side of the conning tower: a turtle. The welcome ceremony took place in one of the U-boat base's pens.

U-203 has crossed the Atlantic from west to east. As a souvenir of catching the turtle, its silhouette has been painted on the conning tower for its arrival in Brest on January 29, 1942. *LB*

U-203's new insignia painted on the side of the conning tower. *UBA*

The coast of Brest is very close; the crewmembers are thinking about how they'll spend their leave once ashore. *UBA*

Commander Mützelburg of U-203 next to the Christmas tree taken on board in December, which has been attached to the *Uzo* binocular support for the arrival in Brest. A lighted garland decorates the tree. *LB*

U-203's welcome ceremony takes place in a double pen at the base. *UBA*

Accompanied by military music played by the brass band on the quay, U-203 enters the U-boat base. *UBA*

The turtle's shell has been fixed on the combat periscope. On the quay in the base, a nurse and female auxiliaries are ready to offer the traditional bouquets of flowers. *LB*

U-203 arrives off the French coast, after a patrol that took it off the coast of Newfoundland. *UBA*

Commander Mützelburg descends to the "winter garden" to salute his Flotilla Chief. U-203 returns from its patrol with four pennants; the one on the bottom represents the silhouette of a warship, the British patrol ship *Rosemonde* that the commander believes (mistakenly) was sunk on January 22. The result is rather small, only two ships have been sunk, the third that had been damaged, was able to reach a port. *UBA*

Then a superior officer of the Army welcomes them home. *UBA*

Chief of the 1st Flotilla, Hans Cohausz, congratulates U-203's crew; a war correspondent records the ceremony with a microphone. *LB*

A nurse has climbed into the conning tower to offer flowers to Commander Mützelburg. We can clearly see the three white pennants for the cargo ships and the red pennant on the bottom for the warship. The tree's garland is lit. *LB*

The day after their arrival, a medal awarding ceremony is organized in front of the former naval school. *UBA*

Chief of the 1st Flotilla Cohausz awards the Iron Cross 2nd Class, notably to the two cadets who have finished their training patrols on U-203: Peter Dönitz on the left and Günter Dobenecker. *UBA*

The crew is presented to the workers. *LB*

In February 1942, about fifteen crewmembers from U-203 are invited to spend three days in Essen, their U-boat's patron town, with a visit to the Krupp factories planned! *UBA*

A party has been organized by the town. Mützelburg has plenty of admirers! *LB*

Kapitänleutnant Mützelburg with his men, in the Krupp factory's "hall of fame." *LB*

During the evening, U-203's crewmembers are invited to stand on their chairs and sing. On February 25, Mützelburg ends their visit with a speech in Essen's largest hall, about the U-boat Corps. *LB*

He accompanies the commander of U-564 to the naval school. *UBA*

Representatives from Essen, notably Mayor Just Dillgardt, have been invited to Brest from March 8-10, 1942. *UBA*

They have a meal with Mützelburg and the Brittany Sector Maritime Commander *Konteradmiral* Gustav Kieseritzky. *UBA*

About fifteen submariners from U-203 were invited to visit the U-boat's patron town of Essen, where they spent three days. Their boat remained in maintenance for six weeks. Watch Officer Hans-Dieter Mohs, present since the first patrol, left to take a commander training course; he later took part in several patrols out of Norway on U-956 and survived the war. Peter Dönitz had also finished his Watch Officer-training course; promoted to *Leutnant zur See*, he was killed along with the rest of the crew when U-954 was sunk on May 19, 1943; Admiral Dönitz lost his second son, Klaus, a year later, killed in combat aboard a torpedo boat in May 1944.

Commander Mützelburg has returned to Brest. While giving his patrol report to Dönitz in Kernével, he is offered a ground job; he refuses the offer as he wishes to continue the war with his crew. He has asked the admiral for a favor: to be sent to the East Coast of the United States for his next patrol. On March 6, 1942, he welcomes his friend Teddy Suhren, who has just returned from a patrol. *UBA*

SIXTH PATROL
FIRST U-BOAT TO BE SUPPLIED AT SEA;
DIRECTION, THE AMERICAN COAST!

After crossing the Atlantic, U-203's watch crew look for U-A, which will be giving them supplies so they can carry out their patrol along the American coast. *LB*

With a new Watch Officer, *Oberleutnant zur See* Hermann Kottmann, and a new Second Watch Officer, *Oberleutnant zur See* Hans Seidel, U-203 left Brest on March 12, 1942. *Leutnant zur See* Hans-Jürgen Haupt was named *Torpedo Offizier* for this patrol. Another officer had also embarked as commander-in-training: *Kapitänleutnant* Hans-Joachim Drewitz, former Chief of the 2nd Mine-sweeper Flotilla, who had volunteered for the U-boat Corps. This patrol was promising; it would be carried out off the American coast where U-boats had obtained good results since the beginning of 1942. On

March 24, between 17:35 and 20:50, after crossing the Bay of Biscay and a large part of the Atlantic, U-203 received supplies in the BC 9555 square from U-A. This was the first resupply mission between two U-boats to be carried out at sea! U-A was commanded by Hans Cohausz, former Chief of the 1st U-Flotilla in Brest! During the following days, U-A also supplied U-84 and U-202 before returning to Norway. At a rate of eight square meters per hour, around twenty-five square meters of fuel was transferred to U-203 that then headed towards a convoy signaled by Otto Ites, commander of U-94.

March 12, 1942: ceremony in the east courtyard of the Brest Naval School for the departure of U-203. Rolf Mützelburg's officers have been changed: the new Watch Officer is Hermann Kottmann, the Second Watch Officer is Hans Seidel. *UBA*

U-203 reverses out of the U-boat base in Brest. *UBA*

On March 24, 1942, U-A arrives! Its commander is Hans Cohausz, former Chief of the 1st Flotilla who had welcomed U-203 to Brest! *YR*

After three hours of resupplying, U-203 is ready to patrol along the coast of the U.S. *YR*

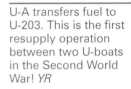

U-A transfers fuel to U-203. This is the first resupply operation between two U-boats in the Second World War! *YR*

A dinghy from U-A is put into the water to transfer foodstuffs. *LB*

The convoy was spotted on March 25 at 09:55. During the afternoon the U-boat maneuvered to get into position in front of the merchant ships that were kept in sight at a distance. Suddenly, at 20:00 a destroyer turned directly towards it! It was only 8,000 meters from the U-boat, which for twenty minutes tried to distance it at full speed on the surface, but the escort ship was faster and finally got dangerously close! At 20:30 the U-boat crash-dived, immediately turning ninety degrees from its route and leaving as fast as its electric motors could go. The destroyer launched thirty depth charges in the spot where the U-boat had been a few moments before. There was an absolute silence on board. After three hours, no sound came from the surface, had it gone? However, at midnight, the escort ship approached at full speed, arriving just over the U-boat stationed at a depth of forty meters and dropped a series of twenty depth charges that exploded nearby. Everything on board was thrown about. The crew believed it to be a particularly experienced British escort ship, certainly not an American one!

U-203 resurfaced at 02:20 on March 26. The damage was repaired but the convoy had disappeared. the U-boat continued its route to the southwest; about 150 miles were covered each day. On March 30, at 18:45 in the CC 1825

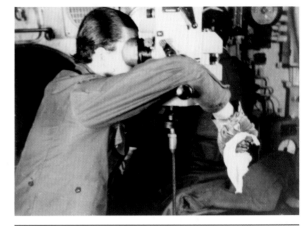

On April 10, a British fuel tanker is spotted. The commander follows it through the watch periscope in the control room. It was sunk by five torpedoes. *UBA*

The tanker, whose crew has been rescued, rests on the surface; it will be towed to a port and repaired. *NA*

On April 11, at 13:20, the American fuel tanker *Harry F. Sinclair* is torpedoed by U-203 and bursts into flame. The U-boat has to dive to escape the destroyer that was escorting it. *NA*

square, the watch crew spotted a rapid steamer heading west. It kept zig-zagging and an attack was judged impossible. On April 1 at 21:50 in the CB 2866 square, a petrol tanker of about 7,000 tons was spotted, heading east. U-203 tried to chase it but visibility was bad, swinging between 300 and 1,000 meters. After searching for fourteen hours, Commander Mützelburg decided to abandon the chase and continue west. In the logbook he wrote: *"A great deception – it was our April Fool!"*

On April 7, 1942, at 10:45, U-203 arrived in the CA 8174 square, in the middle of the East Coast of the U.S. A petrol tanker on fire was spotted near the coast, but U-203 had to dive when a small lookout plane appeared at 11:15. It had to dive once again at 15:00 with the arrival of two four-smoke-stack destroyers looking for the U-boat that had sunk the tanker! The U-boat rested on the seabed with total silence on board!

At 17:00 the commander had just decided to turn on the electric motors to distance the U-boat from the zone, when a plane was seen in the periscope! Three bombs exploded about 3,000 meters away. At 17:30, a fourth exploded just over U-203! The U-boat sank once again to the seabed, at a depth of thirty meters. Decidedly, the sector was well guarded by the planes and the destroyers! U-203 only resurfaced at 02:53 on April 8, and the commander decided to head for Cape Hatteras.

After firing its last torpedo at a British cargo ship on April 14, 1942, the commander drinks a shot of rum out of the silver goblet. He believes that he has sunk five ships during this patrol, but in reality, only three of them sank and the other two were only damaged. *UBA*

The next day at 04:45, torpedo boats passed nearby. The U-boat continued its route at periscope depth. At 21:55, a 6,000-ton petrol tanker was seen in the periscope at a distance of 3,000 meters, sailing at a speed of twelve knots, but it had been discovered too late due to bad visibility and it was too far away to attack. On April 10 at 02:40, the tanker was once again in view, U-203 made approaching maneuvers at full speed. At 03:47, it fired two torpedoes from tubes No.1 and No.2, the tanker was hit by one of them and stopped. The following two torpedoes launched from the tubes No.3 and No.4, didn't explode. The tubes were reloaded and at 05:08 a new torpedo fired from tube No.3 exploded in the middle of the tanker after forty-

Getting ready for their arrival, certain crewmembers have shaved off their beards. *LB*

nine seconds. A second, bigger explosion suddenly blew the ship out of the water – it must have been full of fuel! This was the 8,072-ton British petrol tanker *San Delfino* with a crew of fifty men, of which only twenty-two survived the attack. The following day, April 11 at 13:20, a petrol tanker estimated at 8,400 tons was discovered, escorted by a destroyer and a Coast Guard boat. At 13:25, U-203 fired a torpedo from tube No.3; it exploded on contact with the tanker that burst into flame. The 6,151-ton American tanker *Harry F. Sinclair Jr.* was evacuated by its crew, leaving ten dead out of thirty-six men. However, the tanker, even though it had been badly burnt, was only damaged and remained afloat. It was towed to a port on April 15; repaired, it was put back into service in 1943.

U-203 rested on the seabed after the attack; it had been chased all evening by the destroyer that dropped thirty depth charges. On April 12, at 02:35, the U-boat resurfaced. A large petrol tanker was spotted at 04:25 sailing at 14-15 knots; the U-boat maneuvered at full speed to get into firing position. At 06:26, from a distance of 1,800 meters, it fired three torpedoes from tubes Nos.1, 2 and 4. They missed their target, but Commander Mützelburg thought that one had hit a 5,000-ton cargo ship that was behind the tanker, at a distance of 4,000 meters. Moreover, a distress message from the 5,032-ton cargo ship *Delvalle* was later captured on the U-boat's radio. In reality, this ship had been torpedoed earlier by U-154 commanded by Kölle. The fourth torpedo, fired at 07:06 from a distance of only 800 meters exploded on contact with the tanker that immediately burst into flame. It was correctly identified in the logbook as the 10,013-ton Panamanian petrol tanker *Stanvac*

On the way home, crewmembers make victory pennants. *LB*

The pennant with the number 13,000 with a yellow border represents the 10,013-ton Panamanian petrol tanker *Stanvac Melbourne*, the number 5,000 represents one of the two cargo ships declared sunk. *UBA*

Mützelburg is welcomed to Lorient by the two Flotilla Chiefs of the U-boats based in this port: Günther Kuhnke in the middle (10th Flotilla) and Viktor Schütze on the right (2nd Flotilla). *UBA*

To avoid British mine fields off Brest, U-203 calls in Lorient on April 29; it leaves for Brest the next day, hugging the coast. *LB*

During the call in Lorient, several crewmembers of U-203 relax in the "winter garden," taking advantage of the sun after several weeks under artificial light. *YR*

Melbourne. Of its forty-nine-man crew, forty-eight were rescued. U-203 only had one torpedo left, but it was under the bridge. The U-boat moved away from the coast to transfer it inside.

Once the operation was finished in the early hours of April 13, the U-boat headed back to the coast of Cape Hatteras. After crossing a destroyer, the commander decided to approach the American coast at periscope depth. At the end of the afternoon, two small steamers were spotted and then a large liner too far away to be attacked. On April 14, at 15:15, an attack was carried out against a British cargo ship estimated at 5,000-6,000 tons. The last torpedo was fired at the merchant ship from a distance of 2,000 meters. The commander had the time to watch it sink before ordering a dive to escape from a U-boat-hunter, which launched three depth charges. The ship sunk was the 6,160-ton British cargo ship *Empire Thrush* carrying 5,000 tons of phosphate, 740 tons of TNT and 2,400 tons of lemon pulp. The fifty-five crewmembers survived the attack. U-203 began its return journey; a message was sent to the *BdU* with the result of five ships sunk for a total of 41,476 tons. Once again the truth is very different: only two ships had been sunk for a total of 14,232 tons, two others representing 16,164 tons had only been damaged. After crossing the Atlantic, U-203 arrived in Lorient on April 29, 1942, at 07:15 and left that same evening at 20:00. This detour by Lorient was forced upon the Germans by the British, who had mined all the direct access lanes to Brest.

U-203 finally reached its homeport at 10:00 on April 30, after following the coast. The U-boat with five pennants hoisted on the periscope was welcomed by a crowd waiting on the jetty in front of the U-boat base; nurses offered flowers to the crewmembers. The officers of the 1st Flotilla accompanied the commander and his officers to the former Naval School for a welcome drink. On May 1, a decoration awarding ceremony was organized in front of the Naval School; Commander Mützelburg decorated several crewmembers with the Iron Cross 1st Class. The U-boat remained in maintenance in the base for a month. *Leutnant zur See* Hans-Jürgen Haupt, present since the first patrol, left the U-boat; he became commander of U-665 on July 22, 1942, aboard which he was killed on March 22, 1943. He was replaced on U-203 by *Leutnant zur See* Julius Arp.

On April 30, U-203 approaches Brest. The victory pennants have been affixed to the periscope. *LB*

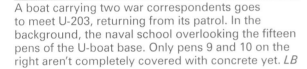

A boat carrying two war correspondents goes to meet U-203, returning from its patrol. In the background, the naval school overlooking the fifteen pens of the U-boat base. Only pens 9 and 10 on the right aren't completely covered with concrete yet. *LB*

A photo of the U-boat is taken from the boat that transfers a port pilot to the U-boat for its approach as well as two war correspondents. In the background, *la pointe des Espagnols*. *LB*

Officers from the 1st Flotilla, one of which is the new Chief Heinz Buchholz (second on the left), are waiting on a platform berthed along the South Jetty. *LB*

German women who work for the Flotilla and a German Red Cross nurse wait for U-203's crew with bouquets of flowers. *LB*

The war correspondents board U-203. While one chats with a crewmember, the other films the U-boat's arrival in Brest. The crew has made five pennants, three with a yellow border representing the patrol tankers, and two others with the number 5,000 representing cargo ships. On the right is the commander's patrolling pennant. *LB*

Mützelburg has received a small bunch of flowers that have been slipped into his buttonhole. *LB*

Chief of the 1st Flotilla Buchholz arrives on U-203's deck to congratulate the crew. *LB*

U-203 in berthing maneuvers; on the left is Commander Mützelburg, next to him is Commander-in-training Hans-Joachim Drewitz. In the background is the U-boat base. *LB*

Mützelburg recounts his patrol to the ground officers. *LB*

Crewmembers chat with the German women who have brought them small bunches of flowers. *LB*

U-203 is put into shelter in the U-boat base. *YR*

Only a war correspondent remains in the conning tower of U-203. *LB*

Preceded by the military brass band, U-203's crew is accompanied to the naval school for the welcome-home meal. *LB*

Commander Mützelburg walks with his Flotilla Chief, Heinz Buchholz. *LB*

A little lower down, Mützelburg's speech on the edge of the sports field. *LB*

Beginning of May 1942, the commander of U-203 gets ready to give a speech to his crew in front of the Naval School. *LB*

Iron Crosses 1st Class are awarded to four crewmembers; strangely, two buttons are missing on the jacket worn by the Marine officer in the center! *LB*

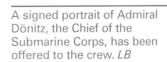

Others receive the Iron Cross 2nd Class. *LB*

A signed portrait of Admiral Dönitz, the Chief of the Submarine Corps, has been offered to the crew. *LB*

SEVENTH PATROL
FIVE ISOLATED SHIPS SUNK IN THE CARIBBEAN; MÜTZELBURG IS AWARDED THE OAK LEAVES

On June 4 in Lorient, the Chief of the 2nd Flotilla greets war correspondent Wolfgang Frank, who boards U-154. In the background, on the left, the conning tower of U-203 which is stopping over. *UBA*

On June 3, 1942, U-203 left Brest at 22:00 for Lorient to avoid the Allied mines laid off Brest. War correspondent Kurt Schulze was aboard the U-boat that left Lorient on June 4 at the end of the day.

It covered about 150 miles a day to reach the CD 5513 square west of the Azores on June 18. Once there, it crossed U-566 commanded by Borchert that was returning from a patrol off the American coast. The two U-boats sailed together towards the CD 5515 square to receive supplies from U-459 XIV-type, commanded by Georg von Wilamowitz-Möllendorf, which they reached at 18:00. At the

On June 3, 1942, U-203 leaves Brest at 22:00 for its seventh patrol; its escort ship accompanies it until 01:30. It follows the coast towards Lorient. *LB*

U-203 has also taken a war correspondent on board: Kurt Schulze, who took this photo of the conning tower, perched on the watch periscope. *LB*

Will the 88mm gun be used this time during a patrol in the Caribbean? *LB*

end of the day, the two U-boats separated, U-566 returned to its base while U-203 continued west. On June 23, in the DE square, the crew celebrated Commander Mützelburg's twenty-ninth birthday. The patrol's monotony was broken two days later at 19:50, when the watch crew in the conning tower spotted a steamer sailing at twelve knots in the DF 1789 square, 450 miles northeast of Puerto Rico. At 23:35, after its approaching maneuver, the U-boat fired a torpedo from tube No.2 from a distance of 2,000 meters and missed!

On June 18, west of the Azores, the XIV-type U-boat transfers supplies to U-203. *YR*

The U-boat resurfaced and advanced to get into a good firing position. On June 26 at 05:44, a second torpedo was fired from tube No.4; it exploded on contact in the middle of the cargo ship. At 05:50, U-203 surfaced alongside its victim, which it had never been able to do before when it attacked heavily escorted convoys in the North Atlantic. The 88mm gun was loaded and fifty-three rounds were fired in thirty minutes at the ship, which sank. It was clearly identified as being the 5,216-ton British cargo ship *Putney Hill*, which was confirmed by the survivors interrogated in their life boats; out of the crew of thirty-eight men, three were killed when the torpedo exploded; the thirty-five others were picked up ten days later.

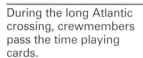

During the long Atlantic crossing, crewmembers pass the time playing cards.

On June 23, 1942, U-203's crew celebrates Commander Mützelburg's twenty-ninth birthday. These German submariners have been given National Navy tropical shirts for the Caribbean sector. On the left: Heinrich Kottmann, the Watch Officer. *LB*

During the morning of June 26, west of the Antilles, U-203 sinks the British cargo ship *Putney Hill* with two torpedoes and fifty-three rounds from the 88mm gun. *LB*

The U-boat continued west; at 20:25, another steamer was spotted in the DC 6512 square. At 23:17, the U-boat attacked, firing a torpedo from tube No.1 that reached its target. This was the 3,666-ton Brazilian *Pedrinhas*, a neutral ship. However, it wasn't flying its national flag and was armed with a 120mm gun. The forty-eight crewmembers aboard lifeboats watched U-203 surface and approach their ship whose rear end was underwater. Two submariners dived and boarded the ship, probably to find papers concerning the cargo. However, they found nothing except a folded Brazilian flag. The ship was then sunk by twenty-two rounds from the 88mm gun.

The U-boat draws away from the ships, which still doesn't sink. *LB*

In the evening of June 26, U-203 torpedoes the Brazilian cargo ship *Pedrinhas*. The cargo ship's crew has taken to the lifeboats. *LB*

U-203 draws alongside the Brazilian ship; two crewmembers board the ship. They don't find any papers concerning its cargo, but they take the flag. *LB*

One after another, the rounds explode under the ship's waterline. *LB*

U-203 returns alongside the ship and the 88mm is positioned to sink it. *LB*

The *Pedrinhas* finally sinks after being hit by twenty-two rounds. *LB*

The U-boat continued its route and approached the Caribbean, a sector where the Allies hadn't yet organized their defenses. On June 28 at 11:15, a third cargo ship advancing at 12.5 knots was spotted in the DC 8732 square. The commander decided to attack at periscope depth to avoid being seen in full daylight. At 15:38 a torpedo was fired from tube No.3 and it hit the ship thirty-two seconds later. This was the 7,176-ton American ship *Sam Houston*, out of Houston for Cape Town and India, carrying 10,000 tons of equipment for the Army. The forty-two survivors out of a crew of forty-six boarded their lifeboats. They saw U-203 that surfaced at 16:00. Watch Officer Hermann Kottmann, former artillery officer on the *Graf Spee*, fired forty-three shells from the 88mm gun to sink the ship. Roland Perry, the commander of the American cargo ship and the Chief Engineer boarded the U-boat for a short while to be interrogated and were then freed. The survivors were picked up two days later. Before this, four other crewmembers died from their wounds. After one of the attacks, a survivor taken aboard the U-boat was offered cigarettes by the crew, which greatly surprised him.

A third ship is sunk in full daylight on June 28: the American cargo ship *Sam Houston*. *LB*

U-203 approaches one of the American ship's lifeboats. *LB*

The American commander and his chief engineer board the U-boat for a few minutes and are allowed to leave. *LB*

The cargo ship is sunk by gunfire; in its hold is 10,000 tons of war equipment bound for Cape Town and then India. Two other ships are sunk during the patrol, which is U-203's most successful. *LB*

U-203 continued its route for the Caribbean. At 00:09 on June 29, the aerial alert sounded for the first time! A second alert sounded at 14:30; the U-boat was at a depth of twenty meters when three well-placed bombs exploded above it. Following the appearance of several other planes, Commander Mützelburg decided to turn round and patrol farther out at sea. On July 4, at 16:00, after several calm days, a radio message from the *BdU* sent U-203 off to Trinidad, south of the Antilles. On July 8 at 04:00 the U-boat was positioned off the port in Trinidad and saw two spotlights. The following day at the end of the afternoon, two cargo ships were spotted, first a small one and then a slightly larger one. The commander decided to attack the second from periscope depth. At 23:05 two torpedoes were fired from tube Nos.1 and 4, and both exploded on contact with the cargo ship which broke in two. This was the 6,914-ton British cargo ship *Cape Verde*, clearly identified in U-203's logbook.

On July 10 at 17:30, a petrol tanker was discovered. An attack was only possible the next day at three in the morning, but the first two torpedoes missed their target. The third, fired at 03:52, exploded on contact with the tanker whose crew climbed into the lifeboats. The fourth torpedo fired at 04:09 sank the ship; this was the 10,013-ton Panamanian petrol tanker *Stanvac Palembang*. U-203 was then chased by an aircraft that dropped a dozen or so bombs in its direction, but as it had dived to forty meters, they didn't cause any damage. The commander sent a radio message with his score for this patrol – for once a real total: five ships sunk for 33,985 tons. On July 15, 1942, the U-boat was on the way home when at 20:00 a message came from the U-boat Corps Command: the Oak Leaves to the Knight's Cross had been awarded to Commander Mützelburg, for having theoretically passed the 200,000 tons of ships sunk.

On July 15, at 20:00, the radioman writes down the message he has just deciphered: the commander has been awarded the Oak Leaves to his Knight's Cross. *UBA*

Rolf Mützelburg is the twelfth U-boat commander to receive this high distinction. Will he now accept the job on land that Dönitz had offered him? *UBA*

The crew prepares for its arrival in Brest. *LB*

On July 23, U-203 received supplies in the DC 2637 square. Aerial alerts started two days later when the U-boat was halfway between the Azores and Spain; before reaching Brest on July 29, seven other alerts were given. When it entered the harbor in Brest, a motorboat brought it garlands of oak leaves to decorate the conning tower, to honor the commander for his new decoration. As well as the pennants made during the return journey, the crewmembers had made a flag with the blazon of U-203 surmounted by the inscription "Mübu" – the commander's nickname, and the Brazilian flag captured from the *Pedrinhas* flew from the top of the periscope. Once ashore, Commander Mützelburg inspected the 1st Flotilla's Honor Company on the jetty in front of the U-boat base.

On July 29, 1942, U-203 approaches Brest, returning from its two-month patrol. The Brazilian flag taken from *Pedrinhas* has been fixed to the top of the periscope. *UBA*

The commander keeps an eye on berthing maneuvers. The three officers from left to right: Hermann Kottmann, Julius Arp and Hans Seidel. *LB*

In homage to the commander's new decoration, the conning tower has been covered in oak leaves brought out on the launch carrying the port pilot and war correspondents. The U-boat's paintwork has suffered a lot during the voyage across the Atlantic. *UBA*

U-203 approaches the South Jetty where the welcome committee is waiting; in the background, the U-boat base and the Naval School. The crewmembers have made a fancy flag with the blazon of Essen (the U-boat's patron town), which has the commander's nickname "Mübu" written on it. *UBA*

Finally, U-203 berths beside a ship moored along the South Jetty. *UBA*

Commander Mützelburg salutes the Honor Company aligned on the jetty and then turns to the group of nurses who are carrying bouquets of flowers. *UBA*

With his friend, Adalbert Schnee, Rolf Mützelburg takes a plane for Germany where both of them receive their new decorations. Schnee has accepted a post on the U-boat Corps General Staff. *UBA*

Rare signed photo of Rolf Mützelburg after being awarded his last decoration. *YR*

War correspondent Arnold Prokop, who had been on U-201, wrote an article about the parallel destiny, up to then, of the two friends Adalbert Schnee and Rolf Mützelburg. *UBA*

Card of the epoch describing the career of Mützelburg, whose motto was *"Hard as Krupp's steel."* His score was twenty-six merchant ships sunk for 178,366 tons, along with a destroyer and an escort ship. Research carried out after the war corrected these results to nineteen ships sunk for 81,961 tons and three damaged for 17,052 tons. *UBA*

On July 30, Mützelburg thanks his crew during a ceremony in front of the Naval School. He then leaves for Paris to give his report to Dönitz. The admiral, who in the past had offered him a job on land, said: *"This time Rolf, it's your last patrol! Lieutenant-Commander Hessler has done a good job as 1st Officer of my General Staff, but he wants to return to the sea, he is going to take your place!"* The commander of U-203 accepts the idea but asks for a favor: one last patrol to have the time to say goodbye to his loyal crew. *UBA*

On August 8, after having decorated several members of his crew in Brest, he waited for the arrival of U-201 commanded by his friend Adalbert Schnee. Both of them had won Oak Leaves for their Knight's Cross on the same day, July 15. They flew together to Germany to receive their decorations. After this seventh patrol, Dönitz tried to persuade Mützelburg to accept a job on land. He was the twelfth U-boat commander to have been awarded the Knight's Cross with Oak Leaves and had become one of the national heroes in Germany where his face was known through the press. The admiral was more insistent this time than he had been in the past; out of four commanders who had wanted to continue the combat after receiving this decoration, three were dead: Günther Prien, Joachim Schepke and Engelbert Endrass; the fourth, Otto Kretschmer, had been taken prisoner. The seven others who had accepted to leave their U-boats, like his friend Adalbert Schnee, had been given responsible positions, notably as Flotilla Chiefs or with the *BdU*'s General Staff, to give new commanders the benefits of their experience.

As to propaganda and recruiting volunteers for the German U-boat Corps, these "Aces" were a much better trump card alive. On the contrary, their loss was always a godsend for Allied propaganda. However, Mützelburg wanted to continue the combat alongside his men; he wanted to carry out one last patrol to have the time to say goodbye to them.

On August 27, 1942, U-203 is ready to leave Brest for its eighth combat patrol. Mützelburg jokes with his loyal Chief Engineer Heinrich Heep, the only officer who has been with him since their first patrol. Watch Officer Hermann Kottmann had been absent during the last two patrols, having been sent to Germany to follow a commander-training course; he had been replaced by Hans Seidel, the former Second Watch Officer. *UBA*

The U-203 left Brest on August 27, 1942. Rolf Mützelburg was the most highly decorated commander to leave for combat. The Watch Officer was *Oberleutnant zur See* Hans Seidel, who had replaced Hermann Kottmann, sent to follow a future commander's course. After four aerial alerts while crossing the Bay of Biscay, a convoy heading south was spotted on September 2 at 14:50 in the CF 2571 square, but it was too fast to be reached and the pursuit was stopped at the end of the afternoon. On September 3 at 15:20, a steamer was spotted. The U-boat approached it, but it was a neutral Portuguese liner. In the early hours of the morning on September 4, U-203 arrived in the CF 8137 square, its operating sector. Until September 9, the U-boat waited in vain for a passing convoy not doing more than twelve miles a day. Then it turned north, arriving in the BE 1448 square.

The Brittany sector Maritime Commander, *Konteradmiral* Ernst Schirlitz, has arrived specially to salute the most decorated German submariner to leave on a combat patrol. After the D-Day landings, Schirlitz was named commander of La Rochelle Fortress. *UBA*

In the early afternoon on September 10, seeing that the crew was bored by the inactivity, the commander allowed his men to go swimming around the U-boat. At 15:00, to set an example, he decided to dive off the conning tower, but the U-boat lurched in the swell and he hit the saddle tanks! He passed out and his neck seemed to have been broken. An hour later, U-203's radio operator sent a message to the *BdU* asking for immediate help. The reply came at 19:00, the U-boat was ordered to the CE 8570 square to meet up with U-462 commanded by Bruno Vowe; this supplier was the closest U-boat to have a doctor on board. Even at full speed, U-203 took a day and a half to reach the rendezvous. Rolf Mützelburg died at 18:00 on September 11. The supply U-boat was spotted in the distance at 10:50 the following day. At 13:35, Dr. Rohrbach boarded U-203 but could only record the death.

U-203 heads for the Azores. The patrol has started badly: during their first dive after leaving Brest on August 27, they found that a super-pressure valve had been tightened with two bolts instead of the usual six; this mistake is immediately corrected. *LB*

Heldentod auf Feindfahrt

Eichenlaubträger Kapitänleutnant Mützelburg zum Gedenken

= Essen, 15. September.

Oft schon ist in den Berichten des Oberkommandos der Wehrmacht der Name des Kapitänleutnants Rolf Mützelburg genannt worden, und immer geschah es im Zusammenhang mit einer ruhmreichen Waffentat im Kampf gegen die feindliche Schiffahrt. Auch der heutige Bericht, der den Heldentod dieses U-Boot-Kommandanten meldet, gibt zugleich einen neuen großen Sieg bekannt, an dem Kapitänleutnant Mützelburg beteiligt war. Die Kriegsmarine verliert in ihm einen ihrer erfolgreichsten und begabtesten

PK.-Aufn.: Kriegsberichter Beuchling (Wb)

Offiziere, die Bevölkerung der Stadt Essen einen Freund, den sie verehrte und liebte.

Rolf Mützelburg wurde am 23. Juni 1913 zu Kiel als Sohn eines Marine-Stabsingenieurs geboren. Nicht nur die Tradition des Elternhauses, sondern auch Temperament, Begabung und Neigung verwiesen ihn auf die seemännische Laufbahn. 1932 trat er in die Kriegsmarine ein. Im Jahre 1936 zum Leutnant zur See befördert, tat er zunächst als Wachoffizier und Kommandant in einer Minensuchflottille Dienst. Im Frühjahr 1941 bekam er ein eigenes U-Boot, das er mit seiner Mannschaft, die er zu einer verschworenen

Gemeinschaft kampfesfroher Männer formte, von Sieg zu Sieg führte. Bereits nach seiner dritten Feindfahrt verlieh ihm der Führer das Ritterkreuz des Eisernen Kreuzes. Kapitänleutnant Mützelburg hatte damals — nach erst fünfeinhalb Monaten des Einsatzes seines U-Bootes — 100 000 BRT. feindlichen Schiffsraumes auf den Grund des Meeres geschickt. Von Unternehmung zu Unternehmung steigerten sich seine Erfolge. Bis Mitte Juli d. J. hatte er 26 Schiffe mit 178 366 BRT. und einen Bewacher versenkt, einen Zerstörer wahrscheinlich vernichtet und weitere Schiffe beschädigt. Am 15. Juli verlieh ihm der Führer in Würdigung seines hervorragenden Einsatzes, der sich unter den schwierigsten Umständen vollzog und die ganze Meisterschaft des Kommandanten zur Entfaltung brachte, als dem 104. Offizier der Deutschen Wehrmacht das Eichenlaub zum Ritterkreuz des Eisernen Kreuzes.

Kapitänleutnant Mützelburg war auch an dem Einsatz deutscher U-Boote gegen die USA. entscheidend beteiligt; er gehörte zu den ersten, die bei diesem Einsatz zum Schuß kamen. Einige seiner Feindfahrten haben unsere Leser durch die Schilderungen von Kriegsberichtern nacherlebt; sie waren reich an Situationen, in denen das Schicksal des Bootes fast besiegelt schien. Immer aber gelang es dem kühnen, zähen Willen und dem überlegenen Können des Kommandanten wie der eisernen Gefolgschaft seiner Besatzung, die Gefahr zu überwinden und das Boot in den Einsatzhafen zurückzuführen, um es zu neuem Kampf und neuem Sieg zu rüsten.

Kapitänleutnant Mützelburg ist wiederholt Gast der Stadt Essen gewesen, einmal auch mit seiner gesamten Besatzung. Er hat unsere Bergleute vor Ort und unsere Rüstungsarbeiter an ihren Werkplätzen besucht, in einer großen Kundgebung vor der Essener Bevölkerung gesprochen. Dabei haben sich viele Bande persönlicher Freundschaft geknüpft, zu der als besonderer Beitrag von seiner Seite ein tiefes Verständnis für den schaffenden Volksgenossen des Reviers gegeben wurde, in dem er den soldatischen Kameraden der Front sah. Die Essener Bevölkerung ihrerseits verehrte in ihm die Verkörperung des deutschen Heldentums, in dem Tapferkeit, kämpferische Begeisterung und Siegeswille mit Lauterkeit, Kameradschaftlichkeit und Schlichtheit zu idealem Einklang kamen.

Nachdem der sterbliche Leib des Eichenlaubträgers Kapitänleutnant Rolf Mützelburg der See übergeben worden war, setzte sein U-Boot die Unternehmung fort. Was könnte eindrucksvoller als diese Feststellung des Berichtes des Oberkommandos der Wehrmacht dartun, daß der Geist Mützelburgs fortlebt in seiner Mannschaft wie im ganzen Nachwuchs der deutschen U-Boot-Fahrer, der Geist des Kampfes, der nur einen Willen kennt: den Sieg!

Funeral aboard U-203 on September 12, 1942, southwest of the Azores. Wrapped in a hammock, covered by a flag and his white cap, lies the body of Commander Rolf Mützelburg, who had been mortally injured the day before when he dived off the conning tower. The U-boat lurched in a sudden swell and his head hit the saddle tanks; unconscious but still alive, he died four hours later. A supply boat with a doctor on board arrived the next day. Watch Officer Hans Seidel takes over the command of U-203. During the ceremony, he makes a speech and the crew of the supply boat salute and fire a salvo of honor.

Article about Mützelburg's death in the German newspapers. *UBA*

When they return to Brest on September 18, a rumor went about saying that U-203's crew had rebelled and thrown their commander overboard! This rumor was perhaps an exaggerated version of a joke spread by some of U-203's crewmembers, who, although they had loved and respected their commander, had jokingly said: *"We didn't sink anything during this patrol, except our commander!"* UBA

A funeral service was organized at 15:12; the supplier fired its two 37mm guns at the moment the dead commander was given to the sea. Watch Officer Seidel, who had taken over the command decided to return to Brest, which was reached on September 18 at 18:00. The crew was sent on leave in two tours; two officers left the U-boat: Watch Officer Hans Seidel (who took the command of U-361 aboard which he was killed on July 17, 1944) and *L.I.* Heinrich Heep, Civil Engineer and *Oberleutnant* in reserve, who was sent to Germany to join the U-boat Technical Development Service to take part in fitting the "*schnorkel*" on U-boats.

U-boat Corps Command, as he could have been saved if he had received immediate treatment: henceforth, all U-boats should have a doctor on board. His testament was found among his affairs in Brest: "*If we don't return from our combat patrol, it will be known that we were doing our duty and that we were ready to give our lives for Germany, for those who will follow after us, and for you who are alive now. As long as people live, there will be wars. My father died a hero's death in combat at sea. Like him, I have done my duty as an officer, with his sacrifice in mind, ready at any moment to give my life like him!*" This testament was reproduced and put up in numerous submariners' hostels.

Rolf Mützelburg: 23 JUNE 1913 - 11 SEPTEMBER 1942

Career:

January 1, 1934:	*Fähnrich zur See*
January 1, 1936:	*Leutnant zur See*
October 1, 1937:	*Oberleutnant zur See*
January 1, 1940:	*Kapitänleutnant*

Decorations:

July 1, 1941:	Eisernes Kreuz II. Klasse	Iron Cross 2nd Class
July 1, 1941:	U-Boots-Kriegsabzeichen	U-boat War Badge
July 1, 1941:	Eisernes Kreuz I. Klasse	Iron Cross 1st Class
Nov 17, 1941:	Ritterkreuz des Eisernen Kreuzes	Knight's Cross
July 15, 1942:	Eichenlaub zum Ritterkreuz	Knight's Cross with Oak Leaves

Ships Hit as Commander of U-203:

Date	Ship	Status	Country	Convoy
June 24, 1941	*Kinross* (4,956 t)		United Kingdom	OB-336
June 24, 1941	*Soloy* (4,402 t)		Norway	HX-133
July 27, 1941	*Hawkinge* (2,475 t)		United Kingdom	OG-69
July 28, 1941	*Lapland* (1,330 t)		United Kingdom	OG-69
July 28, 1941	*Norita* (1,516 t)		Sweden	OG-69
Sept. 26, 1941	*Avoceta* (3,442 t)		United Kingdom	HG-73
Sept. 26, 1941	*Lapwing* (1,348 t)		United Kingdom	HG-73
Sept. 26, 1941	*Varangberg* (2,842 t)		Norway	HG-73
Nov. 3, 1941	*Empire Gemsbuck* (5,626 t)		United Kingdom	SC-52
Nov. 3, 1941	*Everoja* (4,830 t)		United Kingdom	SC-52
Jan. 15, 1942	*Catalina* (632 t)		Portugal	
Jan. 17, 1942	*Octavian* (1,345 t)		Norway	
Jan. 21, 1942	*North Gaspe* (888 t)	damaged	Canada	
April 10, 1942	*San Delfino* (8,072 t)		United Kingdom	
April 11, 1942	*Harry F. Sinclair Jr.* (6,151 t)	damaged	USA	
April 12, 1942	*Stanvac Melbourne* (10,013 t)	damaged	Panama	
April 14, 1942	*Empire Thrush* (6,160 t)		United Kingdom	
June 26, 1942	*Pedrinhas* (3,666 t)		Brazil	
June 26, 1942	*Putney Hill* (5,216 t)		United Kingdom	
June 28, 1942	*Sam Houston* (7,176 t)		USA	
July 9, 1942	*Cape Verde* (6,914 t)		United Kingdom	
July 11, 1942	*Stanvac Palembang* (10,013 t)		Panama	

Score: **nineteen ships sunk for 81,961 tons and three ships damaged (17,052 tons).**

NINTH PATROL
THE SUCCESS OF COMMANDER HERMANN KOTTMANN
IN THE CANARIES SECTOR

*O*berleutnant *zur See* Hermann Kottmann, former Watch Officer during the sixth and seventh patrols, who had been on a commanders' course during the eighth, was named commander of U-203 on September 21, 1942. Apart from the Second Watch Officer, *Leutnant zur See* Julius Arp present since the seventh patrol, the three other officers were new: *Oberleutnant zur See* Helmut Röttger as Watch Officer, *Oberleutnant* Walther Dörholt as Chief Engineer and, after the accidental death of the former commander, Dr. Heinz Schrenk was taken on board. U-203 left Brest on October 15, 1942 at 17:00, for its ninth war patrol. The U-boat had been equipped with a Metox radar detector, which should alert it in the event of approaching Allied planes. It went off four times in two days during the Bay of Biscay crossing.

The U-boat heads for a new sector: the Canary Islands off the African coast. *YR*

On October 15, 1942,
U-203 leaves Brest for
its ninth combat patrol.
Apart from Second Watch
Officer Julius Arp, the
other officers are all new:
Helmut Röttger Watch
Officer, Walter Dörholt
Chief Engineer. *YR*

Hermann Kottmann is named commander
of U-203 on September 21, 1942. He
had served on the pocket battleship *Graf
Spee* at the beginning of the war. After the
ship had been scuttled in the neutral port
in Montevideo on December 17, 1939, he had
been imprisoned in Argentina until July 1940. He
managed to escape to Chile where he took ship
across the Pacific, and reached Germany by the
Trans-Siberian railway. Volunteering for the U-boat
Corps, he took a training course between June and
November 1941, before taking part in two patrols
on U-203 as Watch Officer. He had just finished a
commander-in-training course when he took his new
command. *LB*

Hermann Kottmann's personal garrison cap.
Private collection

On October 25, the watch crew sight three ships: a fuel
tanker escorted by two destroyers. But bad coordination
on board makes firing impossible and the U-boat is chased
by one of the destroyers. *YR*

At 20:50 on October 25, in the DH 4782 square between the Azores and the Canaries Isles, the watch crew spotted three ships sailing east. They were immediately signaled by radio message and the commander decided to attack; approaching, they saw that it was a huge petrol tanker weighing about 10,000 tons accompanied by two destroyers. Due to bad communication between the conning tower and the interior, the torpedoes weren't ready when the ships passed at only 300 meters from U-boat. In addition, the U-boat was spotted by one of the destroyers because it surfaced too soon, only fifteen minutes after they had passed. The destroyer headed straight for it. In spite of dropping their *Bold* sonar decoys, the ship arrived almost on top of the U-boat, which crash-dived. Miraculously, for the U-boat, no depth charges were dropped on it!

When U-203 resurfaced at 23:48, the ocean was empty. However, any pursuit was impossible as the starboard diesel engine didn't work; a pump was out of order. After it had been repaired, the U-boat continued its route south. On October 27, at 16:45, smoke from ships was spotted and the commander decided to attack during the night. At full speed,

In the evening of October 27, U-203 is in a good position in front of a convoy to fire at it. A destroyer turns towards it, but the U-Boat fires off four torpedoes on the surface towards the cargo ships. They all miss their targets. *UBA*

U-203 positioned itself in front of the convoy. At 21:00 three escort ships passed it and Commander Kottmann had several merchant ships in front of him. Just as he prepared to order fire at 22:03, an escort ship suddenly approached the U-boat that was on the surface. Even so, Commander Kottmann decided to fire an emergency salvo of four torpedoes towards the cargo ships, but in the bad conditions, they missed their targets.

U-203 managed to escape at full speed, chased by the escorts that were too far away to fire at it. The commander decided to attack the next day in full daylight. At full speed the U-boat positioned itself once again in front of the convoy at 10:58 and dived to periscope depth. However, when the convoy was 5,000 meters away, it changed course and the attack was a failure. U-203 didn't manage to catch it a third time because of bad visibility. On October

29, at 02:43, in the DH 5142 square southwest of Madeira, the watch crew in the conning tower spotted an isolated cargo ship that had stopped! At 04:52, a torpedo was fired from tube No.1 from a distance of 2,500 meters, adjusted at a depth of two meters. The moon was so bright that the watch crew could follow the torpedo's path; they noticed that it jumped from wave to wave and missed its target!

The starboard diesel engine's pump, which had been damaged, is repaired, and the U-boat can continue on its route. *YR*

Commander Kottmann manages to position the U-boat in front of the convoy the following day. He orders a crash-dive and gets ready to fire when the convoy suddenly changes course. *YR*

The second torpedo, fired at 04:58 from tube No.2 also jumped the waves but exploded on contact with the ship, sending up a cloud of smoke eighty meters high. A light on the hit ship went on and suddenly the U-boat's conning tower was caught in the spotlight only 2,000 meters away and had to crash-dive! At 09:30, U-203 resurfaced to find the ship sinking slowly. The U-boat approached a lifeboat with eighteen men on board; they explained that they had been part of the SL 125 convoy, but they had been left behind because their engines had been damaged; in reality, their ship had been damaged by a torpedo fired from U-509 on October 28. Commander Kottmann had the 20mm gun fire several shells to sink the ship faster. This was the 5,178-ton British cargo ship *Hopecastle* carrying 2,500 tons of magnetite and limonite as well as 3,000 tons of diverse merchandise. Another isolated ship was discovered on October 30 at 03:16 in the DH 2549 square and also seemed to have stopped. U-203 fired a first torpedo from tube No.1 at 03:41 from a depth of three meters; it jumped from wave to wave and missed its target! The same thing happened with the next two.

The fourth, fired from tube No.4 exploded on contact with the ship, sending up a cloud of smoke 100 meters high, but it didn't sink. The U-boat surfaced and sank it with sixty-four rounds from the 20mm gun fired below the waterline. This was the 7,131-ton British cargo ship *Corinaldo* carrying over 5,000 tons of frozen meat. It had also been part of the SL-125 convoy and had been hit by a torpedo from U-509 on October 29 at 22:16; its crew had abandoned it. As it hadn't sunk, two torpedoes had been fired at it from U-659 at 02:07 the following morning before being finished off by U-203 at 10:25. This was the twenty-first and last

In spite of searching with the hydrophone, the convoy can't be found. *LB*

victim of this U-boat. As all its torpedoes had been fired, the U-boat turned back towards its home base. Brest was full and it received the order to go to Lorient, which it reached on November 6 at 11:30. For his first patrol, Commander Kottmann had sunk two ships for 12,309 tons. He and the crew were welcomed by *Kapitänleutnant* Günther Kuhnke, Chief of the 10th Flotilla, who decorated six crewmembers with the Iron Cross 1st Class.

Finally, on October 29-30, U-203 spots two ships that have left the convoy after sustaining damage by other U-boats. The British cargo ship *Corinaldo*, already torpedoed by two U-boats, is the twenty-first and last victim of U-203. The U-boat then turns back towards Lorient. *DR*

On December 6, 1942, U-203 left the berth A3 on the Scorff in Lorient, for its tenth combat patrol. The patrol zone fixed by the *BdU* was the AK 60 square, right in the middle of the North Atlantic. From December 9, problems with the diesel engines, which had to be repaired, forced the U-boat to advance submerged for long periods using the electric engines, which reduced the distance covered to around 100 miles a day for three days instead of the 150-160 miles in normal conditions. A radio message received on December 11, at 21:36, sent it to a new operation sector: the AL 8595 square west of Ireland. The problems with the diesel engines still hadn't been resolved. U-203 reached its zone in the evening of December 13 and joined the *Raufbold* wolfpack to hunt convoys. A steamer was spotted on December 16 at 04:50 but it quickly disappeared into the low-lying cloud. Because of its problems with the Diesel engines, U-203 could only cover about seventy-five miles a day. Weather conditions, already bad, got even worse on December 20 and lookout on the surface was impossible.

U-203 leaves Lorient on December 6, 1942; Commander Kottmann's friends salute him. The U-boat has been nicknamed "*Zirkus Kottmann*" (Kottman's Circus). Is this because of the bad maneuvers and this commander's hesitations during his first patrol, or because of the good atmosphere that reigns within the crew? *UBA*

U-203 is moored on the Scorff in Lorient at the A3 berth, the former transport ship *Isère*. *UBA*

U-203 leaves for its tenth patrol, heading for the North Atlantic. *UBA*

In addition to the blazon of its patron town of Essen and the turtle, a new insignia has been painted on the bottom of U-203's conning tower: the Olympic rings. This is to show that Commander Kottmann graduated in 1936, the same year that the Olympic Games were held in Berlin. *Thierry Nicolo*

The electric engines have to take over from the diesel engines, which slows the U-boat's progress. *UBA*

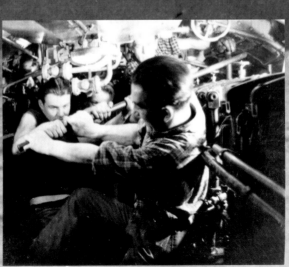

The mechanics take several days to repair the diesel engines, which are finally functional on December 21. *UBA*

After December 9, due to a problem with the diesel engines, the U-boat only covers 100 miles a day. *YR*

The weather conditions have deteriorated, the sea is so rough on December 20 that it is impossible to keep watch on the surface. *LB*

At 23:45 the following day, a radio message ordered U-203 and three other U-boats to turn east to the AK 99 square; they formed the new *Spitz* wolfpack. The mechanics had finally repaired the diesel engines that now functioned normally. An alert was sounded on December 26 at 12:58 – a bomber forced the U-boat to dive three times. During its last flyover, it dropped two series of five bombs in the direction of the submerged U-203, without causing any damage.

On December 28 at 16:45, the watch crew spotted smoke from ships and then their masts in the distance. Two other U-boats were seen, also heading for the merchant ships. At 20:41, the U-boat was close enough to the convoy to fire three torpedoes from a distance of 1,800-2,000 meters, but they jumped over the waves and missed their targets. U-203 was immediately chased by a destroyer but managed to escape at full speed on the surface. At 22:46, returning to 3,000 meters from the convoy, it fired at a large cargo ship estimated at 9,000 tons but had to turn back immediately when a destroyer headed towards it. The crew heard a loud detonation before the U-boat disappeared into the night.

As the rest of the convoy was being attacked by the other U-boats in the wolfpack, the escort ship abandoned the pursuit of U-203. Commander Kottmann decided to attempt a third attack. At 00:50 on December 29, approaching once again to a distance of 800 meters, he gave the order to fire three torpedoes at two cargo ships and a destroyer, but once again, they jumped over the waves and missed their targets. Through the periscope between 06:00 and 09:00, the commander watched a destroyer maneuvering to pick up the survivors from the torpedoed ships. The convoy disappeared the next day.

It was the ON-154 convoy, out of Liverpool on December 18 for New York; it lost fourteen ships out of forty-six, which was considerable, but none of them had been sunk by U-203. On December 31, at 10:18, the radio operator received a message from the *BdU* ordering them to return to base. At midnight, the crew celebrated the New Year at sea.

Brest was reached on January 7, 1943. Once they had landed, several crewmembers were decorated, notably Mechanic Hermann Pickert who, for the exceptional work on the engines, received the DKiG – the German Gold Cross which he had been awarded at sea on December 21, 1942. The U-boat remained at the base for three months undergoing repairs, which gave the crew the chance to take a long leave. Commander Kottmann spent a part of his holiday in a ski resort with his wife. Watch Officer Helmut Röttger left the U-boat for a future commanders' course; he was killed on June 13, 1944, as commander of U-715. He was replaced on U-203 by *Leutnant zur See* Joachim Schmidt-Prestin. Chief Engineer Walter Dörholt also left the boat; he died aboard U-86 on November 29, 1943. He was replaced by the former L.I. on U-86, *Oberleutnant (Ing.)* Friedrich Albutat. For its next patrol, U-203 took on board three officers-in-training: Uwe Brandt, Joachim-Albrecht Neander and Karl Oxfort.

Empty-handed, U-203 turns towards Brest. Weather conditions and engine problems have made this patrol very difficult. Potato-peeling duty. The crew passes Christmas and the New Year on board. *YR*

On December 28, a convoy is spotted. In spite of trying to attack three times, U-203 doesn't manage to sink any ships; its torpedoes are tossed from wave to wave. *UBA*

U-203 arrives in Brest on January 7, 1943, this time without any victory pennants. *UBA*

The U-boat is going to spend three months in the arsenal undergoing a complete overhaul, which means that the crew can spend their leave in Germany. *YR*

The logbook recording the eleventh patrol sank with U-203 on April 25, 1943. However, the patrol had been described in detail by Watch Officer Joachim Schmidt-Prestin who survived the wreck. Returning to Germany in 1946, he wanted to relate, in a letter addressed to the father of Chief Engineer Friedrich Albutat, dead on board, the exact circumstances concerning the death of his son.

Chief Engineer Friedrich Albutat, formerly on U-86, is named the new chief engineer on U-203. *YR*

Before the departure on operation, a party is organized in Brest. The men are very confident; during March U-boats have sunk 108 Allied ships representing 585,404 tons and have damaged twenty-three others; among those destroyed, seventy-one were part of convoys, a record! But the Allies' efforts will soon stop this hemorrhage; the months of April and May will mark a turning point in the Battle of the Atlantic. *UBA*

This photo of U-203's last departure on April 3, 1943 was taken by a war correspondent based in Brest and given to Rosemarie von der Heiden, Chief Engineer Albutat's girlfriend employed by the 1st Submarine Flotilla. *YR*

The new Watch Officer, *Leutnant zur See* Joachim Schmidt-Prestin, who survived the destruction of U-203. Returning to Germany after his imprisonment in the United States, he wrote about the last patrol to give the chief engineer's father the circumstances of his son's death. *YR*

U-203 crosses the Atlantic once again for the coast of Newfoundland. *YR*

On April 25, 1943, the British destroyer HMS *Pathfinder* dropped depth charges on U-203 for four hours, forcing it to re-surface. *DR*

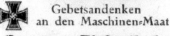

Gebetsandenken
an den Maschinen=Maat

Hermann Tiefenthaler

Träger des EK 1, EK 2 und des
U-Bootkriegsabzeichens

gefallen im April 1943 im Nordatlantik, im blühenden Alter von
22 Jahren.

Auf einem Seemannsgrab
da blühen keine Rosen,
auf einem U-Bootsgrab,
da blüht kein Blümelein.
Der einzige Schmuck das sind
die Meeresrosen und heiße Tränen
die die Heimat um mich weint.

The families in Germany publish the death notices. *UBA*

He wrote: "*Straight after our departure on April 3, 1943, we had a slight setback because of an air raid warning, but nothing happened. We continued on our way safe and sound in the first hours of the evening. The Bay of Biscay crossing, which until then had been very dangerous because of the increased activity of Allied aviation, passed without incident or difficulty. It's true that the weather wasn't favorable for the aviation. After the Bay of Biscay, a little west of the 15th degree, we had our first contact with the enemy, a small steamer. While we were getting ready to attack it, a large liner that we thought must be the Queen Elisabeth suddenly appeared. However, we weren't in a position to attack it with any chance of success and besides, we were forced to dive with the unexpected arrival of a plane, which didn't seem to have spotted us. So we had to abandon our offensive. After that, we headed towards several convoys but without being able to attack any of them. Also we had a rather seriously damaged machine that your son quickly repaired in a very exemplary way.*

He and the others had to work for several hours without stopping. On April 17, we came across another small steamer that we thought was on its own and which could be a godsend. While we were getting ready to attack it, we realized that it was a camouflaged escort ship – but only when it opened fire at us! However, we were able to escape without any damage as we had dived in time. Even its depth charges didn't reach us. While I was on watch duty on Easter Sunday on April 25, on a beautiful day with only a little mist, an aircraft carrier came into view! As conditions were favorable for us to attack it, we decided to get into firing position before the end of the evening to attack it during the night. Everything went well and we had established our plan two hours earlier, when we were discovered by one of the planes and forced to dive. It also dropped a bomb that didn't cause any damage.

Internment index card of a survivor from U-203 at the American prison camp in Papago Park. *UBA*

U-203's memorial plaque at Moltenort with the names of the ten crewmembers who were killed in action. *YR*

The chief engineer is posthumously awarded the Iron Cross 1st Class. *YR*

MtrGfr. Hans Löwenkamp signed this photo while in captivity to send to his family. *YR*

But an hour or so later the British escort destroyer 'Pathfinder' found us and launched depth charges from an engine that we had never seen before and we began to ship water from the rear. In spite of the important amount of water, to our surprise your son managed to keep the U-boat stable. But after about four hours, we reached the point where one more depth charge would destroy us. The commander, after consulting with the officers, decided to surface and scuttle the boat. We surfaced with great difficulty. When the British destroyer saw that we had abandoned the combat, it ceased its initial fire but nevertheless fired several shells under the water level, more for the form of the thing than to sink us.

Your son was still on board with two men to open the diving valves. Usually, this operation didn't represent any danger; it should have been child's play for the three men to get out of the U-boat. But perhaps those last shells had really damaged U-boat, to a point that it sank incredibly quickly. I should add that the escape ladder broke just as the three men tried to get out. The commander leant into the hatchway and really tried to hold onto it, but it was impossible. That's how your son and two other friends were carried to the seabed. It was really a bad blow for all of us, especially as we owed our lives to his exemplary action during the attack."

The interrogation of the survivors and the Allied reports confirmed this description of the facts. After having unsuccessfully chased several convoys, U-203 was discovered on April 25 by a Swordfish taken off from HMS *Biter*. The plane called the destroyer *Pathfinder* that then launched five depth charges before sinking the U-boat with its gun once it had regained the surface. With the Chief Engineer, nine other crewmembers lost their lives. Commander Kottmann and twenty-seven other crewmembers were taken prisoner.

Four crewmembers from U-203 in a U.S. prison camp. *YR*

Zur Erinnerung an unseren Brüder u. Schwager Oberleutnant Jng. Friedrich Albutat
der im April 1943 mit U-Boot 203 im Nordatlantik gefallen ist.

Former Watch Officer Joachim Schmidt-Prestin attached this engraving to his letter to Friedrich Albutat's father, as a souvenir of U-203's last patrol. For several months, the chief engineer's father had hoped that his son was still alive. *YR*

Reunion of the veterans of U-203 at Cuxhaven in 1991. Horst Bredow, founder of the Submarine Archives, is standing. *YR*

BIBLIOGRAPHY
AND SOURCES

The U-203's logbook.

The interrogation of U-203's survivors, American archives, Washington, D.C.

Die Ritterkreuzträger der U-Boot-Waffe, by Manfred Dörr, Biblio Verlag, 1988.

Der U-boat Krieg, vols.1-5; Rainer Busch & Hans-Joachim Roll, Mittler Verlag, 1996-2003.

U-Boat Operations of the Second World War, by Kenneth Wynn, Chatham Publishing 1997.

The Allied Convoy System by Arnold Hague, Vanwell Published Ltd., 2000.

Acknowledgements: Horst Bredow creator of U-Boat Archive in Cuxhaven (†February 22, 2015); Yves Rio who contacted several veterans of U-203 at the end of the 1990s and who kindly allowed me to use the photos and documents he had collected; Thierry Nicolo, and Monique, Alain Durrieu and Lucien Le Pallec (†) for their proofreading. This book it dedicated to the victims aboard the Allied ships sunk by U-203.